The Whole World a Bauhaus

HIRMER

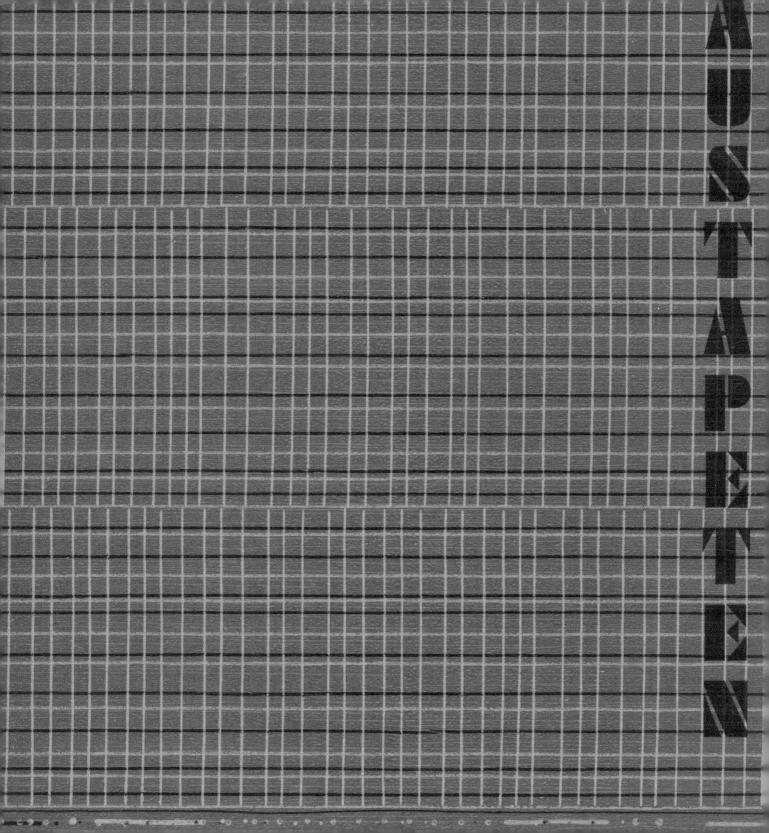

The Spirit of the Bauhaus

Ulrich Raulff
President
Institut für Auslandsbeziehungen (ifa)
Ronald Grätz
General Secretary
Institut für Auslandsbeziehungen (ifa)

The Bauhaus was only in existence for a few years. But in that period and, above all, in the period after the Bauhaus closed down, this art school became a symbol of modernism. The late 1960s marked a highpoint in the influence and critical reception of the Bauhaus. Modernism was celebrated in many large exhibitions, including *Bauhaus: Eine Ausstellung von Idee und Arbeit, von Geist und Leben am Bauhaus 1919–1928 und bis 1933* (Bauhaus: An Exhibition of Thought and Work, of Spirit and Life at the Bauhaus, 1919–1928 and until 1933). The Darmstadt archives were moved to Berlin, where a new organisation, the Bauhaus Archive, was established. At a time when designers and artists were turning away from the avant-garde, the Bauhaus was given a new lease of life by the museums and their systems of memorialising.

No institution has succeeded like the Bauhaus in turning the everyday work of teaching into a way of life. Today, the Bauhaus stands for a state of mind: avant-garde, free, progressive, and modern in the social, political, and artistic senses. The Bauhaus has become a symbol. In spite of all the criticism that began to be voiced in the 1960s, especially about its functional approach, Bauhaus modernism is still a significant point of reference. It has been reassessed and yet returned to the fore as a counter to post-modernism. Art historian Roger M. Buergel, the director of Documenta 12, found a precise formulation for this complicated incongruity in one of the leitmotifs of his Documenta exhibition: "Is modernity our antiquity?"

In 2019, marking the 100th anniversary of the founding of the Bauhaus, we are compelled to reflect on its current relevance. Argentinian architect Tomás Maldonado (1922–2018), teacher and director of the Ulm School of Design from 1955 to 1967, answered this question as follows: "The Bauhaus is only accepted in [a] superficially conservative way. […] After all, this is no more than a mere appearance, an attempt to canonise the Bauhaus, or still better to archeologise it, to transform it into a relic only shown on festival occasions, to transform it into an object of adoration which sometimes fulfils the functions of a totem, sometimes of a taboo."[1] His text, entitled "Is the Bauhaus Relevant Today?", was published in 1963, at a time when the reception of the Bauhaus had reached a peak. In 1960 the Bauhaus Archive was founded in Darmstadt by art historian Hans Maria Wingler (1920–1984), who directed it until his death. The aim of the archive was to conduct research on the Bauhaus and to publish its findings. Through texts, catalogues, and exhibitions, the memory of the Bauhaus was kept alive, securing it a place in the present. On the occasion of the Archive's opening, the *Stuttgarter Zeitung* wrote: "If you want, you can refer everything back to the Bauhaus, and let it shine out into the future from there."[2] Under Wingler, the archive saw itself as the institutional memory, with the task of reflecting on its significance for the present day. Documents were collected, organised, and managed, and it also supported the network of Bauhaus teachers and students who were still alive. Wingler worked very closely with Walter Gropius, and together they were instrumental in shaping the contemporary image of the Bauhaus and the discourse associated with it.[3]

Wingler also organised the exhibition *50 Jahre bauhaus*, together with former Bauhaus master Herbert Bayer (1900–1985), exhibition designer Dieter Honisch (1932–2004), and art historian Ludwig Grote (1893–1974). In 1968, the Institut für Auslandsbeziehungen (ifa) organised a successful tour of this exhibition, sending it to various museums around the world: it was shown in Chicago in 1969, Buenos Aires in 1970, and Tokyo in 1971. The aim of the exhibition was clearly stated in its title, which translates as "50 Years of the Bauhaus"—that is, it defines a period of time much longer than the existence of the school itself, as its ideas continued to thrive decades after its closure. This Bauhaus represented a certain spirit, which had shifted away from simply producing objects toward advancing a specific attitude, one that went beyond the aesthetic design of everyday life. This exhibition, financed by the state of Baden-Württemberg and the German Foreign Office, also had

1   Tomás Maldonado, "Is the Bauhaus Relevant Today?", *Ulm: Journal of the Hochschule für Gestaltung* 8/9 (September 1963), p. 8.

2   Richard Biedrzynski, "Bauhaus: Zur Eröffnung des Darmstädter Archivs auf der Mathildenhöhe", *Stuttgarter Zeitung*, 10 April 1961.

3   "I back him up through thick and thin because he opened his ears to all my advice, and I hope he will go on doing this." Walter Gropius on Hans-Maria Wingler, quoted in Claudia Heitmann, *Die Bauhaus-Rezeption in der Bundesrepublik Deutschland: Etappen und Institutionen* (Trier, 2001), p. 49.

Walter Gropius, Opening of the exhibition *50 Jahre bauhaus*, Württembergischer Kunstverein, Stuttgart; demonstration against the closing of the Ulm School of Design, 4 May 1968

Portuguese edition of the catalogue *bauhaus*, 1974

a cultural and political agenda: to show the Bauhaus as a shining example of a free and democratic German community in the midst of the Cold War and the conflict between East and West—even if this community was at that point already historical. The very idea of the Bauhaus was itself a timeless model that could be applied all over the world, independent of any particular institution. However, the *50 Jahre bauhaus* exhibition made it possible not only to report on the artistic avant-garde but also to take a closer look at the Weimar Republic years, seen as providing the context which made the Bauhaus possible. This was a period open to ideas of democracy and freedom, and thus a positive point of reference for the culture of memory in contemporary West Germany. The Bauhaus was a place where earlier advocates of democracy worked, before their influence was abruptly terminated by the Nazi dictatorship.[4]

In 1969, one year after the exhibition premiered in Stuttgart, Wingler's Bauhaus Archive received an offer of financing from the city of Berlin, which included the construction of new premises and a move from Darmstadt to Berlin. Walter Gropius designed the new building, which was then constructed—with considerable alterations to Gropius's design—between 1976 and 1979. The Bauhaus supporters thus established an institution that to this day works to keep the memory of the Bauhaus alive, in both academic circles and for a general public. From the 1960s on, information about the Bauhaus and its artists and products was collected, researched, and then brought into museum collections; meanwhile, a new generation of designers was becoming more critical. As the memorialisation of the Bauhaus reached a peak, its approach was subjected to deep criticism. Functionalism, with its separation of working and living environments, was in crisis. Classical modernism, which saw itself as a new and timeless movement, was now considered blind to history. Universalism assumed that the achievements of progressive architecture could be implemented anywhere in the world, but this view was now increasingly challenged. How international is an international style, and to what extent can Bauhaus ideas truly be transferred to other cultures?[5]

This is the context that underlies our view of the Bauhaus, which is now ripe for reappraisal.

The exhibition *The Whole World a Bauhaus* intends to draw attention once again to the Bauhaus school, and to show both its diversity and complexity. In just a few years, the Bauhaus attracted designers and artists who revolutionised the first half of the twentieth century—with abstract painting and figurines that jumped from the two-dimensional space of the painting to walking on stage; with experiments in photography and film; with text and font designs that challenged established reading habits; with applied art that was seen as equal to the fine arts; and with teaching methods that were to become a standard model for schools around the world.

Another part of the exhibition focuses on cultural transfer, which not only covers the history of how the Bauhaus was received, but also includes an examination of parallel modernist movements in countries outside Europe. It is presented in eight sections, developed by curators from the specific regions where these movements unfolded. We asked them to consider the question "The Whole World a Bauhaus?" and received responses from Buenos Aires, Casablanca, Mexico City, Moscow, Santiago de Chile, Stuttgart, the USA, and Karlsruhe, where the ZKM | Center for Art and Media has become a byword for the "Digital Bauhaus". These case studies offer multiple perspectives on this twentieth-century artistic movement, with consideration given to the particular circumstances in each area. The focus is not on those who emigrated from Germany after the Bauhaus was closed in 1933, but rather on the spread and use of Bauhaus ideas and related transcultural contexts in the 1920s. In 1925, for example, the Chilean artist, composer, and musician Carlos Isamitt (1887–1974) came to Europe in order to study teaching, and he then implemented the methods he had learned when he founded the Escuela de Bellas Artes in Santiago de Chile. Even the thistle drawn by students in Johannes Itten's preliminary course was integrated into the curriculum there, but no longer as a synaesthetic study. Instead, the aim was to use it as an abstract pattern with indigenous forms. The spirit of the Bauhaus provided the impetus, but it was transformed into something else. A project of this kind can only be undertaken by many people working together. We would

50 Jahre bauhaus, Museo Nacional de Bellas Artes, Buenos Aires, Argentina, 1970

like to thank the artistic director of the exhibition, Valérie Hammerbacher (ifa), the curator of the touring exhibition Boris Friedewald and the curators of the regional contributions, Enrique X. de Anda Alanís, Silvia Fernández, Margret Kentgens-Craig, Alexander Klee, Salma Lahlou, David Maulen, Christiane Post, and Peter Weibel. We also thank Ilke Penzlien, Peter Kortmann, Lina Grumm, and Annette Lux for the exhibition design. We thank Peter Weibel, Philipp Ziegler, and Hannah-Maria Winters for their willing cooperation, which enabled us to present the exhibition at the ZKM | Center for Art and Media in Karlsruhe. We hope that exhibition visitors will experience the spirit of the Bauhaus together with us in this exhibition—"in productive disunity", as painter Josef Albers described the Bauhaus community of masters in 1922.

4   Claudia Heitmann, "Die Ausstellung '50 Jahre bauhaus': Kulminationspunkt der bundesdeutschen Rezeption", in ibid., pp. 224–38.

5   On this, see Rasheed Araeen, "Our Bauhaus: Others' Mudhouse", *Third Text: Critical Perspectives on Contemporary Art and Culture* 3, no. 6 (1989), pp. 3–14. See also the exhibition *Magiciens de la Terre*, 18 May 1989 – 14 August 1989, Centre Georges Pompidou, Paris, and also the polemic text by Tom Wolfe, *From Bauhaus to Our House* (New York, 1981).

50 Jahre bauhaus, Museo Nacional de Bellas Artes, Buenos Aires, Argentina, 1970

Christian Dell
Teapot, nickel silver, silver, ebony, 1922
Private collection

Tubular steel furniture, Wagenfeld lamps, and Marianne Brandt's teapot—today, these are the objects most commonly associated with the Bauhaus. A living and working community that continuously sought to redefine itself, the Bauhaus was open to a wide range of design approaches in addition to its famous form-finding processes. This teapot with ebony handle is probably one of the first objects to be made at the Bauhaus by the twenty-eight-year-old silversmith Christian Dell. It reveals much of the craftsmanship and personal touch that Dell brought with him when he became manager of the Bauhaus metal workshop in January 1922. The body of the teapot, which sits on four playful little feet, at first seems bulbous, but then resolves into a crisper, slimmer form distinct from the rest. The large, flat shoulder area is fluted, and it almost seems as if the lid is a ball that has plopped into the water, producing visible waves. The ebony handle resembles a drop of water. In this way, Dell takes a somewhat playful and humorous approach, allowing the idea of water to resonate in his design on multiple levels. The pot, however, is also representative of the objects produced by the metal workshop in terms of its handcrafted character. It was only in the autumn of 1922, when Gropius asked Dell to shift his focus to prototypes for industrial mass production, that the design slowly began to change. Oskar Schlemmer, who had become master of form in the metal workshop that same autumn, also had a clear idea of the direction in which the design could develop: "We can become pioneers of simplicity."

Boris Friedewald

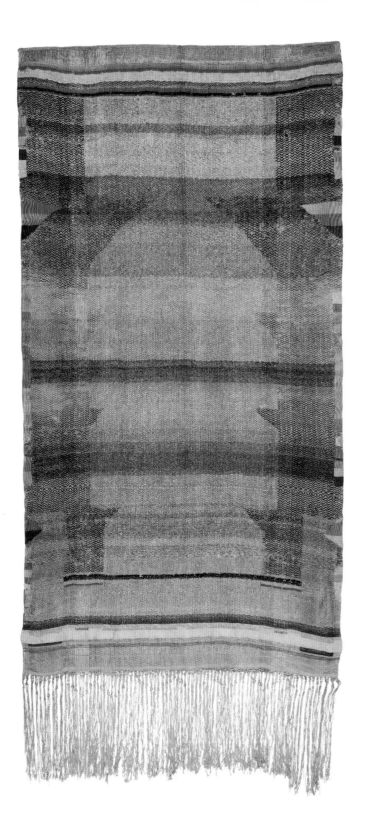

Anonymous
Wall hanging, twill weave with twisted warp,
silk, dyed woollen lining, cotton, synthetic silk,
c.1923
Private collection

When we look at the carpet, we see what appears to be a faraway place cradled in the colours of an early-morning haze. The centre of the wall hanging has a radiant quality, as if one were looking through a window behind which delicate shades of golden ochre, pink, and purple are laid on top of one another in a variety of nuanced combinations. It is impossible to know whether the association with architectural forms was deliberate: in any case, to create this wall hanging, the anonymous artist used colours and structures in deliberately subtle ways. The piece, which was presented during the Weimar Bauhaus exhibition in 1923, subsequently went missing, and for a long time it was only known from black-and-white illustrations. The pictorial space is layered not only vertically—in the direction of the weave—but also perpendicularly, creating an imaginary sense of depth.

As one can see, the weft is handled in two different ways, such that the narrow borders with brightly coloured block stripes are visually distinct from the rest of the worked surface. This amplifies the sense of oscillation between foreground and background. In the borders, the weft threads were inserted in the traditional tapestry style: in the horizontal direction, they run alternately above and below the vertical warp, and in the next row, the other way around. Pushed together firmly one on top of the other, they form a compact colourful surface that is noticeably ribbed. The sheen of the yarn further intensifies the colour. In the larger part of the tapestry, on the other hand, the weft threads were run over two or more warp threads and the individual rows were left loose, so that the light-coloured warp threads could also stand out and form a pattern. A horizontal zigzag picture is created, whose shimmer covers almost the entire surface.

Judith Raum

Fritz Kuhr
Wohnsiedlung (Housing Estate), watercolour,
brush drawing, 1925
Collection of Hermann Famulla

Not every building that the Bauhaus painters committed to paper or canvas reflected the utopian visions being discussed at the school. And yet, as motifs for painting, the houses and cities were inextricably linked to the constant discussions on the future of dwelling, living, and building that involved all the students and teachers. There can be little doubt that this dynamic inspired the painters at the Bauhaus to create free associative works on paper and canvas. Paul Klee's *Dream City* from 1921 shows an urban scene created entirely from the imagination. The twenty-four-year-old painter Fritz Kuhr saw this painting when he travelled to Weimar for the major Bauhaus exhibition in 1923 on the recommendation of artist Otto Pankok. Kuhr was so fascinated by Klee's work that he enrolled at the Bauhaus in 1924. After attending the preliminary course, he decided to train in the wall-painting class, which was first run by Wassily Kandinsky as master of form and later by the young master Hinnerk Scheper, after the school moved to Dessau in 1925, the year in which Kuhr produced his *Wohnsiedlung* (Housing Estate). This work may have been inspired by the urban development projects planned by the Bauhaus in Dessau. In his almost graphic representation of small and large residential buildings—the gabled roofs betray the conventional concept of architecture behind them—Kuhr appears to be primarily concerned with visualising and emphasising colour surfaces and geometric figures composed of rectangles and triangles. The picture may also contain a gentle criticism of a past form of architecture that was unable to cater to the features that the housing designs of the Neues Bauen movement sought to provide for everyone: living in glass architecture and on balconies offering light, air, and sun.

Boris Friedewald

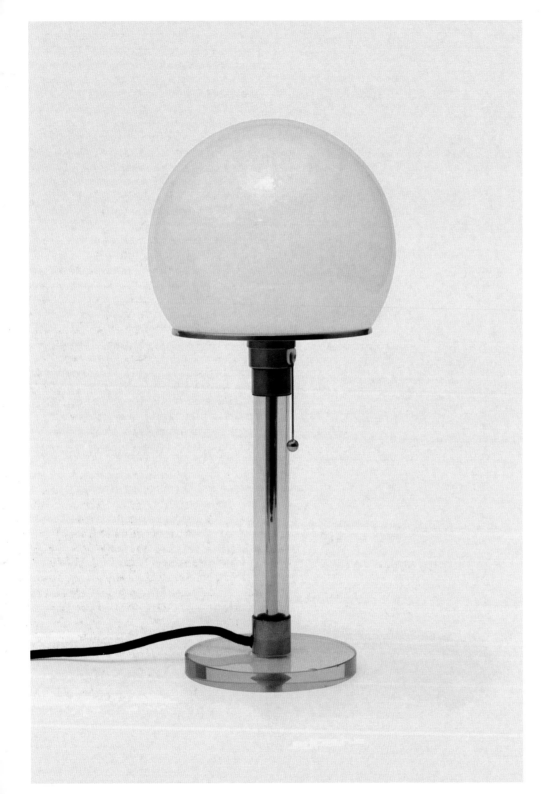

Wilhelm Wagenfeld
Table lamp, opaline glass, glass/metal base
painted matte black, nickel-plated brass,
fabric-covered flex, Architekturbedarf
Dresden W2 and W1 design, 1930
Collection of Christoph Wowarra

The so-called Wagenfeld lamp, in its different versions with metal or glass base, is perhaps now seen as *the* flagship product of the Bauhaus workshops, a byword for progressive modernism with an affinity for technology.
In 1924, Wilhelm Wagenfeld gave a matter-of-fact description of its austere form: "A round plate, a cylindrical tube, and a spherical shade are the lamp's most important elements."[1]
A native of Bremen, Wagenfeld had been admitted as a student to the Weimar Bauhaus in 1923 and attended the metal workshop run by László Moholy-Nagy. Inspired by Moholy-Nagy, he designed the metal model of the lamp in 1924 and eventually supplemented this with a model in glass. Carl Jacob Jucker, who had come to the Bauhaus from Switzerland, was the first to experiment with lamps made of glass, and the integration of this material into the shaft of Wagenfeld's model can thus be attributed to him.
From 1925 on, the model types ME1 and ME2 were manufactured by the Bauhaus GmbH company, which had been established in Dessau, making them one of the first products in the Bauhaus range. Although the school's original aim was to strive toward the modern ideal of industrial manufacture, this was abandoned in favour of manual production, which was still a complex undertaking. In the same year, Wagenfeld patented an improvement to the glass model and worked on the technical development of both models until 1930. The W1 and W2 designs were then manufactured by Architekturbedarf Dresden.
The Wagenfeld lamp was a symbol of modernity, yet it was this association that led to its downfall in 1933, at which point its production was halted. It was not until 1979 that Wagenfeld and the Tecnolumen company relaunched it in a slightly modified form. Since then it has been copied regularly. Although its scanty output makes it relatively unsuitable as a desk light, its sculptural quality and timeless elegance still make it attractive for use in the home.

Elisa Tamaschke

1   Quoted in Magdalena Droste,
*Die Bauhaus-Leuchte von Carl
Jacob Jucker und Wilhelm
Wagenfeld* (Frankfurt am
Main, 1997), p. 22.

KOGA

VOL.2 NO.12 1933

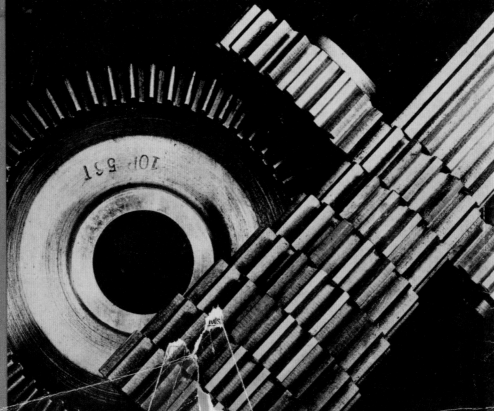

光画

山脇巌

KOGA, vol. 2, no. 12, 1933
Collection of Institut für Auslandsbeziehungen

The December 1933 issue of the Japanese photo magazine *KOGA* contains an essay on photomontage as developed by Kurt Kranz at the Bauhaus Dessau. Edited by photographers Kozo Nojima, Iwata Nakayama, and Ihei Kimura from May 1932 to December 1933, *KOGA* was a platform that brought European photography to Japan. *Ko* means "light" and *ga* means "image",[1] and thus, as the name suggests, it was dedicated to the modernist program such as it was outlined, for example, in László Moholy-Nagy's 1929 statement in the Werkbund magazine *Die Form*: "and indeed, this is the problem facing optical design in the future: the design of direct light."[2] *KOGA* also transforms the Werkbund magazine's typography: the typeface of the uppercase letters, the placement of the name, the colour bars, and the greenish-blue colour create a complementary effect. The *KOGA* cover you see here bears the dedication "1939 — for Kurt Kranz" and the note "by Yamawaki Iwao". Yamawaki, who was himself a student at the Bauhaus from 1930 to 1932, reports in this issue on Kranz's work in the Dessau photography course and advertising department. He focuses on photomontage and links the dismembered figures Kranz cut out of magazines and mounted on pieces of paper to collages by Moholy-Nagy.[3] For Yamawaki, it is the elements of dance and improvisation expressed in Kranz's figures that give the work coherence:[4] photographic realism is dissolved by movement. The photographer's eye, which is identified with the camera in El Lissitzky's montage on the cover of the issue of *Die Form* referred to above, translates the technical image into the optics of art.

Robin Rehm

DIE FORM
ZEITSCHRIFT FÜR GESTALTENDE ARBEIT
4. JAHR
HEFT 10   15. MAI 1929
VERLAG HERMANN RECKENDORF G.M.B.H. BERLIN W 35

1   I am grateful to Dr Takagi Akira from the department of philology and literature at Kyoto University for his editorial and bibliographical input.

2   László Moholy-Nagy, "Fotogramm und Grenzgebiete", *Die Form* 4 (1929), pp. 256–9, here: p. 258.

3   On Kurt Kranz's interest in practices of decomposing the image, see Christian Spies, Raster, "Eine Infrastruktur des Sehens", in Robin Rehm and Christoph Wagner (eds.), *Designpatente der Moderne: 1840–1970* (Berlin, 2019), pp. 398–404.

4   I would like to thank Dr Yabuta Junko from the institute of art history at Kobe University for translating Yamawaki Iwao's *KOGA* essay into German.

Franz Singer
Tubular steel chair, 1932–1934
Collection of Gerald Fingerle

1   Gustav Adolf Platz, *Wohnräume der Gegenwart* (Berlin, 1933), p. 430; on Marcel Breuer's B33, see Otakar Máčel, "Marcel Breuer: Inventor of Bent Tubular Steel Furniture", in Alexander von Vegesack and Mathias Remmele (eds.), *Marcel Breuer: Design and Architecture* (Weil am Rhein, 2003), pp. 52–114.

2   Platz's foreword was written in March 1933 and thus provides a *terminus ante quem* for Singer's tubular steel chair: Platz, *Wohnräume der Gegenwart*, p. 8. A wire model of Singer's chair is shown in reproduction in Elena Makarova and Friedl Dicker-Brandeis, *Ein Leben für Kunst und Lehre: Wien, Weimar, Prag, Hronov, Theresienstadt, Auschwitz* (Vienna/Munich, 2000), p. 88.

3   Platz, *Wohnräume der Gegenwart*, p. 150.

4   Patent Specification, No. 462381, Provisional Specification, Franz Singer, Improvements relating to Chairs, Tables, Stands and like Furniture, Application Date: June 6, 1935, Specification Accepted: March 8, 1937, pp. 1, 33–36.

5   Ibid., pp. 1, 37.

6   Platz, *Wohnräume der Gegenwart*, p. 150.

7   German Reich Patent Office, Austrian Branch, Nr. 156087, Franz Singer in Vienna, Tubular Metal Furniture and Processes for Its Production, registered on 9 December 1936, term of patent starts 15 December 1938, issued on 10 May 1939, p. 2.

8   Platz, *Wohnräume der Gegenwart*, p. 66.

"F. Singer: Easy-to-assemble steel armchairs" reads architect and author Gustav Adolf Platz's caption to the photograph of a stack of three metal chairs made by Franz Singer, the shape of which is based on Marcel Breuer's B33, produced by Thonet from 1928/29 onwards.[1] The criss-cross runners of Singer's chair—which can probably be dated to 1932—are the main feature that distinguishes it from the model it was derived from.[2] Starting from this basic form, Singer developed a system that, as Platz describes, made it possible for "the pieces of furniture to be pushed into one another for transport and storage".[3] On the basis of this, Singer obtained a patent in England in 1935. "In accordance with my invention," the specification states, "I provide various alternative constructions, all possessing the feature that close nesting is possible."[4] In the case of the tubular steel chair in question, it is the cross in the frame formed by the design of the runners—"the first form of construction" for Singer—that permits this nesting.[5] Singer's tubular steel chair includes yet another innovation: when Platz talks about an "elastic seating set-up in a concise form",[6] he is referring to the elaborate mounting of the textile seat and backrest: they are stretched between two steel-strip flanges mounted on the tube by means of pegs, a construction that allows the seat and backrests to be re-tensioned when they become slack and pulled up in line with the upper segments of the tube wall. "Through this re-tensioning," Singer notes in another patent application submitted in Austria in 1937, "the fabric can be brought to the height of the plane tangential to the top of the tubes, so that a tightly stretched wall is created above the tubes."[7] The rocking experienced when sitting, the space-saving stacking system, and the guarantee of taut fabric panels to accommodate the body weight are described by Platz as a "compaction of functions".[8]

Robin Rehm

Bauhaus Artists between Abstraction and Empathy: Wilhelm Worringer's History of World Art
Valérie Hammerbacher

"I've just been reading Worringer's *Abstraction and Empathy*. He has a fine mind that we can certainly use. A wonderfully skilled line of reasoning, concise and cool-headed, extremely cool in fact."[1] In Wilhelm Worringer, the painter Franz Marc—co-founder of the editorial association Der Blaue Reiter—saw an ally, or indeed a translator capable of turning the artistic language of expression into a conceptual language of science. In 1923, he recommended the book to his friend Wassily Kandinsky. August Macke had drawn Marc's attention to the work back in 1911: "Franz, do you know Worringer's book *Abstraction and Empathy*? I read it and found parts of it really exquisite. There's a great deal in it for us."[2] On 30 July 1911, Paul Klee made the following observation in a letter to his wife, Lily: "[Worringer] is in favour of the distance between nature and art, regards art as a world unto itself, does not think that the primitives were lacking in skill, etc. I have long seen everything as an achievement, but as a scholarly statement it is highly gratifying."[3] In his diary, Johannes Itten summarised his reading of *Abstraction and Empathy* by taking quick notes, accompanied in each case by references to the text: "Aesthetic pleasure is objectified self-indulgence! Functional purpose, raw material, and technology are the coefficients of friction in the overall product, together with artistic volition." He then drew the following conclusion for his own work: "I must contain the space even more, so that everything is as closed as it is in my room. Every form is also very clearly specified without any randomness. The ancients made everything as two-dimensional as possible, because the spatial order could only be described indirectly through intersections and reductions. It is colour that allows me to confer space directly. To be redeemed from the randomness of being human in the contemplation of something essential, immutable."[4] Illumination, self-alienation—there are a great many Bauhaus artists who felt that the text spoke to them.[5] But what kind of book was it that elicited such enthusiasm from its readers and earned the author the title "Father of German Expressionism"? Wilhelm Worringer (1881–1965) had succeeded in formulating a manifesto for contemporary, modern art that also took non-European cultures into consideration. In classifying the evolution of art, what concepts did he work with such that many found their work validated—so much so that he was invited to the Weimar Bauhaus on 5 January 1921 to give an art historical lecture with the simple title "The Ancient Portrait"? By that time, *Abstraction and Empathy* was already in its tenth edition.

In 1907, Worringer completed his doctorate in art history at the University of Bern, where he came to know Reinhard Piper through their collaboration on a Lukas Cranach biography. Piper's publication of Worringer's dissertation, *Abstraction and Empathy: A Contribution to the Psychology of Style*, in 1908, represented a triumphant first step for his work, which codified what many contemporary artists had been focusing on in the years prior to World War I. It was a book that became increasingly popular with each new edition—one in which the avant-garde recognised its own artistic volition and aesthetic discourse, even seeing Worringer as an accomplice in the field of scholarship.[6]

Worringer's work was not an artistic manifesto, nor did it explicitly include works of contemporary art. *Abstraction and Empathy* deals with art history, systematising—from the perspective of psychology and the theory of perception—the evolution of art from antiquity to the Renaissance. His investigation is based on the act of volition that finds expression in every artistic work. Worringer quotes extensively from two works by Alois Riegl, who inspired him to think of the work of art as an independent organism that has no relation to the objects found in nature.[7] It is the will, not the ability, of artists that should be examined, and thus the true condition under which a work of art is created. He saw the work as an autonomous creation that was articulated in two ways: through naturalism and style, which characterised the individual works. Both are expressions of an experience of the world. This experience is characterised on the one hand by empathy, and on the other by a desire for abstraction. Or, as Worringer put it, "These two poles are only gradations of a common need, which

1 Helga Grebing, *Die Worringers: Bildungsbürgerlichkeit als Lebenssinn. Wilhelm und Marta Worringer (1881–1965)* (Berlin, 2004), p. 35.

2 Ibid. p. 35.

3 Felix Klee (ed.), *Paul Klee, Briefe an die Familie, 1893–1940* (Cologne, 1979), vol. 2, p. 786.

4 Writing in Vienna on 5 December 1917, Johannes Itten quoted pages 75, 77, and 85 from the first theoretical part of Worringer's work; Eva Badura-Triska (ed.), *Johannes Itten: Tagebücher* (Stuttgart, 1913–16; Vienna, 1916–19; Vienna, 1990), unpaginated.

5 Anni Albers acknowledged that the book had been an illumination for her. Nicholas Fox Weber, *Die Bauhaus-Bande: Meister der Moderne* (Berlin, 2019), pp. 409–10. Ludwig Hilberseimer's essay "Schöpfung und Entwicklung" was based on the writings of Wilhelm Worringer, in *Der Einzige* 1 (1919), pp. 4–6; Frank Jüttner, *Ludwig Hilberseimer und das Primitive in der Kunst* (Stuttgart, 2018).

is revealed to us as the deepest and ultimate essence of all aesthetic experience: this is the need for self-alienation" (p. 23). While abstraction finds "beauty in the life-denying inorganic, in the crystalline" (p. 4), artists who empathise with the world celebrate the living. Abstraction is a mechanism for coping with the contingency of an environment perceived as threatening, confusing, and chaotic. It manifests itself in the liberation of the individual form, which negates any three-dimensionality and only extends in the two dimensions of height and breadth or articulates itself in patterns, especially in ornament. Worringer's pair of contrasting terms not only enabled him to describe "Graeco-Roman and modern Occidental art" (p. 8) but also offered a way of getting to grips with previously excluded areas of art production, "the artistic creations of many ages and peoples" (p. 8), the evaluation of which had hitherto been a hopeless task. The character of these styles, which had previously been viewed negatively, and their idiosyncratic qualities were cast in a new light by the analysis of the specific psychological conditions governing them. They were not inferior to classical European art, but merely different, far removed from the description of them as the "charming, childlike stammering of stylisation" (p. 44), as one art historian had dismissed them in his foreword to the Vienna Genesis. "Thus all valuations made from our standpoint, from the point of view of our modern aesthetics, which passes judgement exclusively in the sense of the Antique or the Renaissance, are from a higher standpoint absurdities and platitudes" (p. 13). Worringer reorganised and resystematised art history by no longer accepting the mimetic quality, the representativeness and imitation of the objects of nature as a criterion for classifying art. Although the "wish to copy" (p. 28) has existed for just as long and sometimes simultaneously with the desire to create, it was not developed from a psychological need and a "feeling about the world" (p. 13) and was therefore not part of art as an autonomous entity and the artist's own aesthetic system. His model of art history revolved around two poles, which are juxtaposed with an evolutionary sequence of styles. It is not the gathering strength of an idea—abstraction, for example—that is radicalised in the course of intellectual

history; rather, the respective poles vary in intensity, sometimes stronger, sometimes weaker, depending on the artists' relationship to the cosmos. The various forms of artistic volition do not manifest in linear fashion, but rather cyclically. For this reason, Worringer can also juxtapose the "lifeless form of a pyramid" with the "suppression of life that is manifested, for instance, in Byzantine mosaics" (p. 14). Worringer's view of evolution is problematic: despite all the appreciation for the beauty of art from different cultures, it is structured in a multi-stage model. Within the various developmental phases he posits, the pre-modern human is said to lack any spiritual or intellectual penetration and to be driven by an instinctual approach to problem-solving. Ancient Egyptian art as a manifestation of Oriental art often served as an example for him. Although several millennia separated him from Egyptian antiquity, people in the modern age were again experiencing a sense of helplessness when faced with the abundance of phenomena while lacking the ability to overcome it with art, unlike the artists of antiquity. In drawings produced in ancient Egypt, preference was given to the surface depicted in terms of planar relationships. "It may be stated here, in anticipation, that of all the ancient cultural peoples the Egyptians carried through most intensively the abstract tendency in artistic volition" (p. 42). They managed this by pressing a three-dimensional body into the surface, thus creating the impression of a plane. "The perfect example of the Egyptian artistic volition is represented by the pyramid, which may equally well be regarded as a sculptural memorial or an architectonic shape. Here the aforesaid tendencies are made most severely and unequivocally manifest, and it is therefore understandable that no other people has imitated this form" (p. 90). Because it was intended to serve as a burial chamber, a cubic building was required, which also had an impact from a distance as a geometric shape. From whatever side one looked at the pyramid, it invariably appeared as an isosceles triangle whose sharp outline precluded an experience of three-dimensionality. The three-dimensional cubic form was translated into an impression of different planes. The actual task of creating a space for a tomb became of secondary importance

6   August Macke's wife wrote, "At long last an academic who engages with these new ideas with understanding and an open mind, who might perhaps champion and defend them against so many of the art historians with their conservative mindsets who have rejected out of hand whatever is new and unfamiliar, without even taking the time to explore it," Elisabeth Erdmann-Macke, *Erinnerungen an August Macke* (Frankfurt am Main, 1987), p. 286.

7   Wilhelm Worringer, *Abstraction and Empathy: A Contribution to the Psychology of Style*, trans. Michael Bullock (Chicago, 1997), p. 44.

Johannes Itten, proportional study of Egyptian art in his diary, before the entry on 14 September 1915

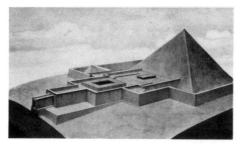

8. GRABDENKMAL DES KÖNIGS SAHU-RE.
MODELL DES TOTEN-TEMPELS UND DER
PYRAMIDE

9. SOMMERHAUS AUS SEELAND (DÄNEMARK)

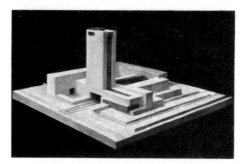

10. MODELL ZU DEM ZENTRAL-FLUGHAFEN
IN BERLIN VON H. KOSINA

Wilhelm Worringer, plate from *Ägyptische Kunst. Probleme ihrer Wertung*, Munich, 1927

Karl Peter Röhl, design for the Bauhaus signet
"Staatliches Bauhaus Weimar", 1919–1921

compared to the planar dimension. Worringer saw in this an expression of all the demands of the desire for abstraction.

The first Bauhaus logo designed in 1919 by Karl Peter Röhl, the winner of a student competition, shows this flat pyramid. It is borne aloft by a "star manikin". The pyramid is reduced to a geometric figure, and only the tapering horizontal stripes create some sense of depth. It is part of an aggregate of signs symbolising different world cultures brought together in the "star manikin" signet. In the centre is the human being, whose outstretched arms and legs touch the surrounding circle of writing, which reads "Staatliches Bauhaus Weimar". It evokes Leonardo da Vinci's *Vitruvian Man*. But having made the allusion to European art history, Röhl did not stop there but augmented the figure with symbols from world cultures: the head of the figure is a circle, one half of which is black and the other white. Yin and yang meet the sun-wheel, a symbol of luck in Buddhism that rotates under the manikin's left arm. It is connected by a curving line that runs across the figure and ends in a rune.

Worringer dedicated the 1927 volume *Egyptian Art* to the art of the Nile valley: "Egypt is the greatest instance of the oasis in the history of the world."[8] His vision of Egypt did not duplicate the orientalist views that describe this civilisation as instinctive, irrational, and passive, but rather focused on its high degree of technological prowess. He takes as an example the harnessing of the Nile floods and the realisation that they could benefit agriculture, seeing therein a transformative power that he equated with that of the modern engine designer, developing propulsion from a destructive explosion. In much the same way, the Egyptians used the catastrophic process of flooding as a means to maximise fertility for agricultural cultivation. Their actions showed the triumph of human intelligence over the forces of nature. Practical usage, a formulaic approach, and a sense of rationalism were characteristic features of this civilisation, which lived on "engineered desert soil". It was matter-of-fact and prudent, intellectual through and through, but without any mystical introspection, akin to the USA. "Here again we find everywhere in parentheses the word 'America'" (p. 15), wrote Worringer when he

elaborated on the rational and spiritual practices of the Egyptians.

Images were interspersed loosely through this publication, and when he focused on Egyptian art in the second chapter, he showed the funerary monument of King Sahure, putting it in a sequence with a functionalist summer house in Zealand, Denmark, and the model made by architect Heinrich Kosina in 1924 for Tempelhof airport in Berlin. The building in the model is made up of blocks positioned in layers above and next to each other, with a tower standing in the centre. All the elements have flat roofs—a prime example of the New Building movement in the mid-1920s, in which space developed from cubature. The same photograph had already been published in 1925 in volume 1 of the Bauhaus Books entitled *International Architecture,* edited by Walter Gropius and László Moholy-Nagy. Worringer concluded with the following assessment: "To make clear that the absolute certainty and clarity of its character has really something to do with what we call Americanism in architecture, we may set side by side the model of an Egyptian temple and pyramid group and a country house in the modern universal style or a model of a modern aerodrome" (p. 24). Further on in *Ägyptische Kunst*, Worringer showed a picture of a grain elevator, which he identified as Canadian. He used an image that Le Corbusier had put in his 1922 book *Vers une architecture* and that Walter Gropius had also used in his lecture "Monumentale Kunst und Industriebau". In 1911, Gropius was invited to the Museum Folkwang by Karl Ernst Osthaus to talk about the contexts in which new forms of architecture were developing. In this lecture, Gropius made explicit reference to Worringer, taking industrial architecture as a specific example of his aesthetics and cultural theory:

"In fact, the architect today applies himself with the same interest to terminal buildings and utilitarian structures as to the other traditional challenges in construction. [...] Thus, in all probability, the blossoming of a new monumental architecture will take as its starting point the enormous tasks posed by technology and industry. Industrial buildings have an innate sense of originality and might residing in them. Power, strictness, and concision are consistent with the organised activity that takes place

8   Wilhelm Worringer, *Egyptian Art*, trans. Bernard Rackham (London, 1928), p. 4. In the previous paragraph he writes, "The striking constancy of character of the Egyptian people has always been remarked upon. This is its explanation: it is not a constancy of blood or race or of a peculiar formation of ethnographical type; it is a constancy in that levelling power of transformation inherent in the conditions of existence peculiar to Egypt" (p. 3). He applies the term "Oriental" with all its pejorative implications to the Hamitic cultures, for example.

there. They have the preconditions for monumentality.

"On the basis of this assumption, allow me to mention first some conceptual prerequisites of a general nature relating to monumental art—which to some extent connect up with Riegl and Worringer's new educational ideas in art theory—as a benchmark for subsequent observations." [9]

He also explained the ordering of chaos through artistic volition, rhythm, and the laws of art, which stem from the mastery of matter.

"The value of the work of art consists only in the satisfaction of an inner desire for redemption, not, for example, in the value of the material. For its creator and beholder, the work of art involves a moment of respite from the confusion of the world view. The wrenching of what is transient from time and space. The artist conquers matter."

Like Worringer, he emphasised the immense size of the buildings as an artistic achievement. Beside the picture of the grain elevator stood the note "An artist evidently worked here."

The grain elevator reappeared in Worringer's *Ägyptische Kunst*, but this time it was to establish a relationship between ancient Egypt and modernism. Here, too, monumentality was the key term denoting a new artistic quality of architecture. It is gigantic, colossal, and at the same time an expression of supreme rationality and abstraction—all characteristics that Worringer described in his cultural model as belonging to "Americanism".

"Here again we may cite for comparison America, where, for example, in architecture (in so far as it has grown out of American actualities, as in industrial buildings, factories, and grain-elevators, and does not appear in the dress of imitation European styles as a cosmopolitan cultured language devoid of character), a greatness and decisiveness of practical construction has developed which is artistically of the highest value, and has rightly become the standard for the architecture of new Europe, that is, of Europe under limitations which are no longer *historical* but *technical*." [10]

For Worringer, grain elevators and factories were derived from functionality:

"To express it in a rough and ready manner—this American power of formation is lack

of imagination. For this reason its form is the highest form of objective rationality. Objective rationality is also undoubtedly one of the most impressive sides of *Egyptian* architecture." [11]

Crucial adjustments had been made between 1911 and 1927 to the image of the elevator. For one thing, in Gropius's lecture, it was thought to have come from South America (p. 134), while by the time Worringer used it in his book, the assumption was that it originated in Canada. For another, in Gropius's notes it still had three small triangular gables rising above the huge bins. By the time Worringer showed the picture, it had been retouched and the gables had disappeared. This made the analogy much easier, because the triangular gable was a typical stylistic feature of antiquity and classicism. This historicist element stood in contradiction to the kind of functionalist geometric flat-roofed buildings found in ancient Egyptian tombs and modern industrial architecture. Worringer was evidently more interested in using the illustration to support the logic of his argument than in checking its validity. This clearly shows how the reference to non-European works of art was generated. There was a desire to see oneself in the other, even if this resulted in a paradox: the path to one's own door led via a detour into the unknown, absent from scholarly analysis either from a personal or from a non-European perspective. The contexts of knowledge were created by the European museums, which preserved the artefacts and presented them in their own categories. Often the scholarly analysis was also based on a reconstruction, since the original archaeological sites were only discovered as ruins.

The reference to anonymous architecture, pile dwellings, Mexican stepped pyramids, Asian round temples, ornaments from India and Java, and distant epochs made this aesthetic detour via the unknown possible for the artists of the avant-garde. For Worringer, it was the Egypt of the Old Kingdom (2680–2180 BCE) and in particular the tomb of Sahure, the second pharaoh of the fifth dynasty, who reigned from 2490 to 2475 BCE. This was a modernism that saw and defined itself, unconditionally and internationally, as a global style and often sought the answers for an art of the future in the creations of a far-distant

9   Quoted in Karin Wilhelm, *Walter Gropius: Industriearchitekt* (Wiesbaden, 1983), p. 116.

10   Worringer, *Egyptian Art*, p. 23.

11   Ibid., p. 24.

21. TORBAU DES TOTENTEMPELS DES KÖNIGS SAHU-RE

22. GETREIDESILO IN KANADA

Wilhelm Worringer, plate from *Ägyptische Kunst. Probleme ihrer Wertung*, Munich, 1927

past—as art historian Richard Hamann summed it up in 1922 in his *Art and Culture of the Present*: "History also takes whole cultures and cultural areas, human eras, and national characteristics in order to construct world history as a unity, like a monument built of cyclopean blocks. Once again, architecture emerges as a leading art form, one that shapes our life today and turns those things that seem not to comply with regular form—such as factories, railway stations, and department stores—into monuments, so that they often stare at us like the pyramids of Egypt, at once huge and adorned."[12]

12   Richard Hamann, *Kunst und Kultur der Gegenwart* (Marburg, 1922), p. 6.

The Bauhaus Workshops
Nicole Opel

This diagram visualises the development of
the Bauhaus workshops under the three
directors Walter Gropius, Hannes Meyer and
Ludwig Mies van der Rohe at the three
Bauhaus locations in Weimar, Dessau, and
Berlin. The work of the specialist form and work
masters is presented chronologically, showing
frequent changes and renaming of the
workshops and the different focus of Bauhaus
teaching under the three directors.

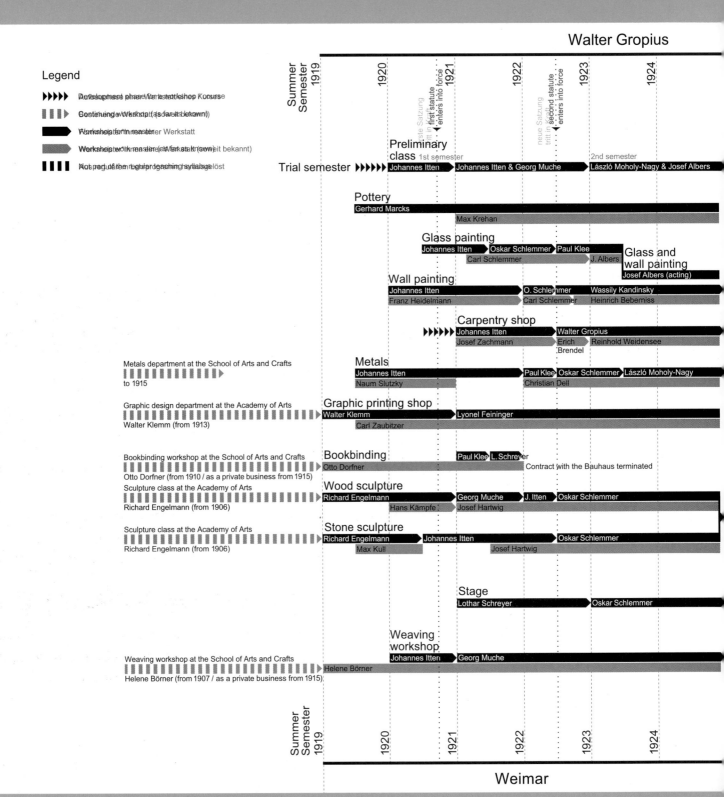

Legend

▶▶▶▶ Development phase Werkstattshop Kuruse / Entwicklungsphase Werkstatt Kurse
▮▮▮▷ Continuing a Werkstatt (as far as known) / Bestehende Werkstatt (soweit bekannt)
◼◼ Workshop for/in master / Werkstatt mit Form- und Werkmeister
◼◼ (grey) Workshop with master (Werkstatt) (soweit bekannt)
▮▮▮▮ Not regular teaching syllabus aufgelöst

Walter Gropius

Summer Semester 1919 | 1920 | 1921 | 1922 | 1923 | 1924

erste Satzung tritt in — first statute enters into force
neue Satzung tritt in — second statute enters into force

Trial semester ▶▶▶▶

Preliminary class — 1st semester / 2nd semester
Johannes Itten | Johannes Itten & Georg Muche | László Moholy-Nagy & Josef Albers

Pottery
Gerhard Marcks
Max Krehan

Glass painting
Johannes Itten | Oskar Schlemmer | Paul Klee
Carl Schlemmer | J. Albers

Glass and wall painting
Josef Albers (acting)

Wall painting
Johannes Itten | O. Schlemmer | Wassily Kandinsky
Franz Heidelmann | Carl Schlemmer | Heinrich Beberniss

Carpentry shop ▶▶▶▶
Johannes Itten | Walter Gropius
Josef Zachmann | Erich Brendel | Reinhold Weidensee

Metals
Johannes Itten | Paul Klee | Oskar Schlemmer | László Moholy-Nagy
Naum Slutzky | Christian Dell

Metals department at the School of Arts and Crafts ▮▮▮▮▷ to 1915

Graphic printing shop
Walter Klemm | Lyonel Feininger
Carl Zaubitzer

Graphic design department at the Academy of Arts ▮▮▮▮▷ Walter Klemm (from 1913)

Bookbinding
Otto Dorfner | Paul Klee | L. Schreyer — Contract with the Bauhaus terminated

Bookbinding workshop at the School of Arts and Crafts ▮▮▮▮▷ Otto Dorfner (from 1910 / as a private business from 1915)

Wood sculpture
Richard Engelmann | Georg Muche | J. Itten | Oskar Schlemmer
Hans Kämpfe | Josef Hartwig

Sculpture class at the Academy of Arts ▮▮▮▮▷ Richard Engelmann (from 1906)

Stone sculpture
Richard Engelmann | Johannes Itten | Oskar Schlemmer
Max Kull | Josef Hartwig

Sculpture class at the Academy of Arts ▮▮▮▮▷ Richard Engelmann (from 1906)

Stage
Lothar Schreyer | Oskar Schlemmer

Weaving workshop
Johannes Itten | Georg Muche
Helene Börner

Weaving workshop at the School of Arts and Crafts ▮▮▮▮▷ Helene Börner (from 1907 / as a private business from 1915)

Summer Semester 1919 | 1920 | 1921 | 1922 | 1923 | 1924

Weimar

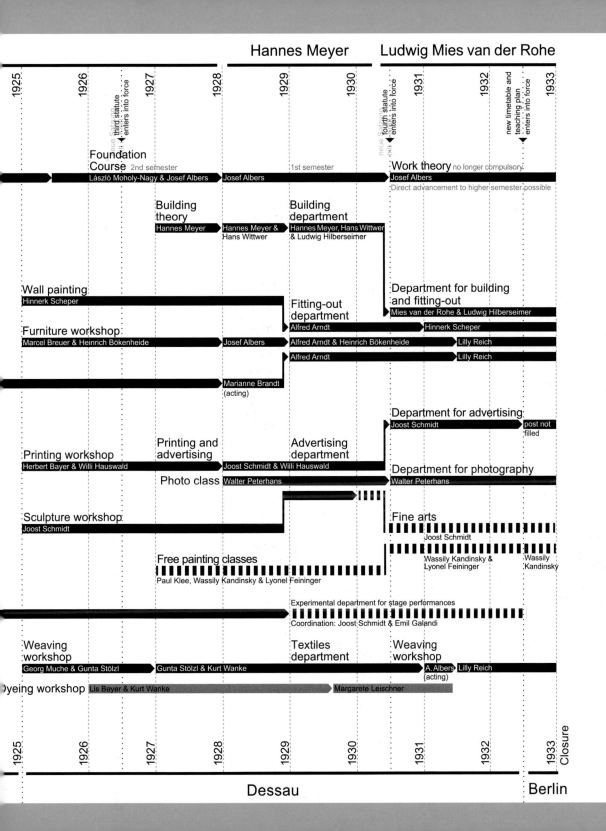

Hannes Meyer   Ludwig Mies van der Rohe

1925 1926 neue Satzung third statute enters into force 1927 1928 1929 1930 neue Satzung fourth statute enters into force 1931 1932 new timetable and teaching plan enters into force 1933

Foundation Course 2nd semester   1st semester   **Work theory** no longer compulsory
László Moholy-Nagy & Josef Albers | Josef Albers   Josef Albers
Direct advancement to higher semester possible

Building theory   **Building department**
Hannes Meyer | Hannes Meyer & Hans Wittwer | Hannes Meyer, Hans Wittwer & Ludwig Hilberseimer

Wall painting   **Department for building and fitting-out**
Hinnerk Scheper   Mies van der Rohe & Ludwig Hilberseimer

Fitting-out department   Hinnerk Scheper
Alfred Arndt

Furniture workshop   Josef Albers | Alfred Arndt & Heinrich Bökenheide | Lilly Reich
Marcel Breuer & Heinrich Bökenheide   Alfred Arndt | Lilly Reich

Marianne Brandt (acting)

          Department for advertising
          Joost Schmidt   post not filled

Printing workshop **Printing and advertising** **Advertising department**
Herbert Bayer & Willi Hauswald | Joost Schmidt & Willi Hauswald   **Department for photography**
Photo class Walter Peterhans   Walter Peterhans

Sculpture workshop   **Fine arts**
Joost Schmidt   Joost Schmidt

Free painting classes   Wassily Kandinsky & Lyonel Feininger   Wassily Kandinsky
Paul Klee, Wassily Kandinsky & Lyonel Feininger

Experimental department for stage performances
Coordination: Joost Schmidt & Emil Galandi

Weaving workshop   **Textiles department**   **Weaving workshop**
Georg Muche & Gunta Stölzl | Gunta Stölzl & Kurt Wanke   A. Albers (acting) | Lilly Reich
Dyeing workshop Lis Beyer & Kurt Wanke   Margarete Leischner

1925 1926 1927 1928 1929 1930 1931 1932 1933 Closure

Dessau   Berlin

On the Path to a Transnational Bauhaus Network

Boris Friedewald

1. The Bauhaus portfolios Neue Europäische Graphik (New European Graphics), the Internationale Architekturausstellung (International Architecture Exhibition) from the first Bauhaus exhibition, and the series of Bauhausbücher (Bauhaus Books)

The Bauhaus made various efforts to develop a transnational network, working together with artists, architects, scholars, art dealers, gallerists, curators, collectors, and well-known individuals in art and culture. It thus attempted to cultivate the image of a "universally intellectual movement"[1] and a global avant-garde community that went beyond the immediate activity of the Bauhaus. This went hand in hand with the Bauhaus's general goal of building its international recognition. With this as its focus, the importance of three Bauhaus initiatives will be addressed here: the Neue Europäische Graphik portfolios published by the Bauhaus from 1922 onward, the Internationale Architekturausstellung in conjunction with the Bauhaus exhibition in Weimar in 1923, and the series of Bauhausbücher from 1925 onward. From these three projects, a circle was formed of notable individuals connected to the transnational artistic, cultural, and architectural avant-garde. Most members of this circle knew each other from the Sturm movement, the Workers' Council for Art, the November Group, and the personal network of Bauhaus masters that was established in the era of Walter Gropius (1919–1928). During the directorships of Hannes Meyer (1928–1932) and Ludwig Mies van der Rohe (1932–1933), the masters and their network also shaped the extensive and multifaceted work of the Bauhaus "internally", as well as the image of the Bauhaus "externally". The fifth section of this essay offers brief portraits of some of the important individuals working within this extended network.

2. The Foundation Stone: The Neue Europäische Graphik portfolios

With the series of Bauhaus portfolios entitled Neue Europäische Graphik, published by the Bauhaus from 1922 to 1924, the school strove to draw attention to its work in a more ambitious way. The advertising brochure for the 1921 project read: "Within the first two years of the Bauhaus, we created the foundation that we deemed correct. In order to be able to do this in all aspects, we kept ourselves—as far as possible—away from the public at large, at the risk that the silence of our work might lead to a misjudgement of the purpose of our endeavours." And further: "All those who do not yet know and cannot know about the work of the Bauhaus shall be made aware of us by this publication."[2] In fact, however, the portfolios only presented the "work of the Bauhaus" to a very limited extent. Only the works in the first portfolio, in which the form masters were represented—plus the lithography and the manual printing press production in the printing workshop, as well as the design of the portfolios—showed this work directly. The brochure promoted the series as an "international collection of graphic works" and declared: "But now we turn to the public with a document that will show how the generation of artists of our time participates in the ideas of the Bauhaus […]".[3] Seventy-five artists were presented, including artists from Germany, France, Belgium, Italy, the Netherlands, Switzerland, Spain, Norway, Austria, Poland, Russia, Czechoslovakia, and Hungary. Their planned contributions were anticipated as "the approval and self-sacrificing cooperation of an entire generation of German and non-German artists" and as a "demonstration of the artists of our time for the idea of the Bauhaus".[4] Although the portfolio presented little of the "work of the Bauhaus", it conveyed much of how the Bauhaus wished to be perceived and how it was to work from then on: as a cosmopolitan community and gathering place of the transnational artistic avant-garde. At the same time, this project was an effective foundation stone—in German, der Grundstein, which was the title originally planned for the series—for a network of transnational artists that was constantly being cultivated and expanded by the Bauhaus.[5] After the nationalism of the

1   See: "Aufruf des 'Kreises der Freunde des Bauhauses'", 1924, in: Volker Wahl (ed.), Das Staatliche Bauhaus in Weimar. Dokumente zur Geschichte des Instituts 1919–1926 (Cologne–Weimar–Vienna, 2009), pp. 325f., here p. 325 [translated].

2   Advertising brochure for the edition of "Bauhaus-Drucke. Neue Europäische Graphik" (Bauhaus Prints. New European Graphics), 1921, in: Klaus Weber, "'Zu Ehren unserer Sache'. Das Mappenwerk 'Neue Europäische Graphik'", in: idem. (ed.), Punkt. Linie. Fläche. Druckgraphik am Bauhaus, exhib. cat. Bauhaus-Archiv Berlin, Museum für Gestaltung, 1999/2000 (Berlin, 1999), pp. 22–33, here p. 23 [translated].

3   Ibid., p. 23 [translated].

4   Ibid. [translated]. The complete text of the advertising brochure is reproduced in: Hans M. Wingler, Die Mappenwerke "Neue Europäische Graphik". Die künstlerische Graphik des Bauhauses (Mainz/Berlin, 1965), pp. 20–2.

5   Gropius initially wanted to title the series "Der Grundstein. Eine Sammlung Europäischer Originalgraphik in fünf periodischen Mappenwerken, herausgegeben vom Staatlichen Bauhaus/Weimar" (The Foundation Stone. A Collection of Original European Prints in Five Periodical Portfolios, published by the State Bauhaus/Weimar); see: Klaus Weber, Punkt. Linie. Fläche (Berlin, 1999), pp. 23f.

First World War, the Bauhaus consciously adopted an alternative concept characterised by open-mindedness and cosmopolitan thinking.

After the first portfolio, which was published in 1922, a "French" portfolio with artists born or living in France was planned. Pablo Picasso, Henri Matisse, and Georges Braque had been asked to make contributions to this second portfolio, but they did not reply, although their names had already been included in the advertising brochure. Others, such as Albert Gleizes, Charles-Édouard Jeanneret (Le Corbusier), and Amédée Ozenfant, had accepted but did not submit their works in time. The launch of this portfolio was thus delayed and only published in 1924, and then in a fragmentary form. The third portfolio from 1922 and the fifth from 1923 both contained works by "German artists". The fourth portfolio, published in 1924, was dedicated to artists born or living in Italy and Russia.

The selection of artists included in the portfolio was apparently not based on any claim to thoroughly present all the trends of the visual avant-garde. Nevertheless, the Bauhaus showed a variety of currents of the European avant-garde with this series, with 110 copies of each portfolio coming onto the market. Thus, for the first time, the Bauhaus also communicated to the public that it did not stand for any one concrete style.

3. Expansion: The *Internationale Architekturausstellung*, 1923

With the major Bauhaus exhibition held in Weimar in the summer of 1923, the aim was to present its works and goals to the world, offering its first comprehensive presentation of the school's achievements. The goal was for critics to be convinced, new orders to be secured, the financially desolate situation to be improved, and the Bauhaus to be made known to wider circles. The international press and notable individuals in art and culture were invited. In the brochure, designed and written by Oskar Schlemmer, he explained how the Bauhaus now wished to be understood: "[…] the history of the Bauhaus becomes the history of contemporary art".[6] However, it became clear that the exhibition should not only present works from the preliminary course, the masters, and the workshops—as Schlemmer suggested that an international art exhibition with "outstanding artists from Germany and abroad" should also be presented to the world as a special show within this framework.[7] In the spring of 1923, the plan was rejected, and the decision was made to exhibit only paintings and sculptures by students and masters in the galleries of the Landesmuseum in Weimar.[8] Nevertheless, the large Bauhaus exhibition was supplemented by an *Internationale Architekturausstellung*, a special show put together by Gropius. After all, the Bauhaus had begun with the goal of a new architecture that artists and craftsmen would create together. In fact, however, only the newly built model house of the painter and Bauhaus master Georg Muche, the Haus Am Horn, was open to the public. In the *Internationale Architekturausstellung*, not only works by members of the Bauhaus were shown, but also by other architects from Germany and abroad. This enabled the Bauhaus to underscore its original goal of increasingly positioning itself as an integral part and gathering place of the transnational architectural avant-garde. In addition to works by the Bauhaus members Muche, Wolfgang (Farkas) Molnár, Adolf Meyer, and Gropius, the exhibition also presented drawings, photographs, and models by avant-garde architects from Denmark, Germany, France, the Netherlands, and Czechoslovakia, as well as by the American Frank Lloyd Wright.[9] There was also a plan to exhibit "new city plans of Moscow and Petersburg, models and drawings of industrial buildings, workers' houses, etc." by Constructivist architects from Russia.[10] Ultimately, though, the participation of Russian architects, who were not mentioned by name, did not come to fruition. The *Internationale Architekturausstellung* received significant praise by the press—even abroad. The newsletter of the Hungarian Association of Architects and Engineers, for example, wrote: "Nearly all the important campaigners of the new architecture come together here for the first time."[11]

4. Development and Integration: The *Bauhausbücher*

In 1923, the Bauhaus came up with the idea to publish a series of *Bauhausbücher*, which it would edit and which were to be published between 1925 and 1930.[12] With this series, the Bauhaus supplemented its image as a gathering place and part of a transnational avant-garde by taking up not only artistic, but also scientific and technical themes. In the first advance announcement of the series, to be edited by Gropius and Moholy-Nagy on behalf of the Bauhaus, it was stated that "experts from various countries who consciously endeavour to integrate their specialised work into the totality of contemporary phenomena of life" had been invited to cooperate.[13] This was a groundbreaking step for the institution, which the Friends of the Bauhaus put forward as a definite plan in its first appeal in 1924: that is, to understand the Bauhaus as a "universally intellectual movement".[14] Of the roughly fifty volumes originally planned, only fourteen were ultimately published. Among the authors were Bauhaus members such as Adolf Meyer, Klee, Schlemmer, Moholy-Nagy, and Kandinsky. Walter Gropius had written the first volume of the International Architecture series. He was not the only Bauhaus member to mention artists and architects from the portfolio series and the *Internationale Architekturausstellung* in his publication and to present their works in illustrations. A glance at the lists of planned themes and authors reveals that the editors, the Bauhaus masters László Moholy-Nagy and Gropius, also drew on artists and architects who had already appeared in or been designated for the *Neue Europäische Graphik* portfolios or who had participated in the *Internationale Architektur-ausstellung*, in their considerations for authors. For this reason, we can speak here of a conscious intensification of networking with a transnational avant-garde, which should and could position the Bauhaus globally as a "universally intellectual movement".

With this project, however, the network built up by the Bauhaus was able to expand even further. Beyond the artists included in the *Neue Europäische Graphik* portfolios and the architects featured in the *Internationale Architekturausstellung*, there were others

6   In: Staatliches Bauhaus in Weimar, "'Die erste Bauhaus-ausstellung in Weimar', Prospekt zur Bauhaus-Ausstellung, Weimar 1923", in: Ute Brüning (ed.), *Das A und O des Bauhauses. Bauhauswerbung, Schriftbilder, Drucksachen, Ausstellungsdesign*, exhib. cat. Bauhaus-Archiv, Berlin, 1995; Württembergischer Kunstverein, Stuttgart, 1996; Gerhard-Marcks-Haus, Bremen, 1996 (Leipzig 1995), pp. 64–5, here p. 64 [translated].

7   "Vorschläge für die geplante Bauhaus-Ausstellung Sommer 1923, Weimar, 15.9.1922", in: Volker Wahl (ed.), *Die Meisterratsprotokolle des Staatlichen Bauhauses Weimar 1919 bis 1925* (Weimar 2001), pp. 234–5, here p. 235 [translated].

8   Ibid., p. 507, note 291 [translated].

9   A complete list of all participants is not yet available. Portfolio 19, "Bauhaus Weimar, Dessau, Berlin", contains an overview of those architects who were represented in the exhibition with "drawings and photos". A further overview can be found in: "Werbeblatt zur Bauhaus-Ausstellung in Weimar vom August 1923", in: Volker Wahl (ed.), *Das Staatliche Bauhaus in Weimar. Dokumente zur Geschichte des Instituts 1919–1926* (Cologne/Weimar/Vienna 2009), pp. 300–2, here p. 301.

10   Walter Gropius in a letter to Erwin Redslob, dated 8 May 1923; quoted in: Klaus-Jürgen Winkler, "Das Staatliche Bauhaus und die Negation der klassischen Tradition in der Baukunst. Die Architektur-ausstellungen in Weimar – 1919, 1922, 1923", in: Hellmut Th. Seemann and Thorsten Valk (eds.), *Klassik und Avantgarde. Das Bauhaus in Weimar 1919–1925* (Göttingen 2009), pp. 261–84, here p. 276 [translated].

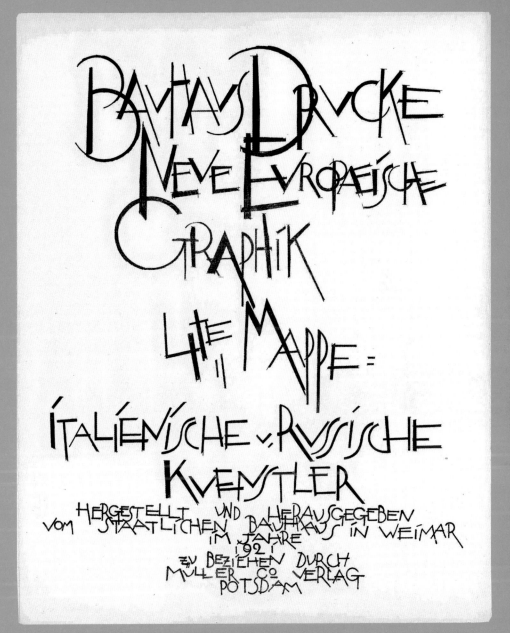

Lyonel Feininger, cover of the portfolio *Bauhaus Prints: New European Graphics. Masters of the State Bauhaus in Weimar*, 1921

László Moholy-Nagy
(typography / cover);
Albert Gleizes,
Bauhausbücher no. 13,
Munich, 1928

Staatliche Bildstelle, Berlin, *Internationale Architekturausstellung* in conjunction with the Bauhaus exhibition in 1923, drawings, photos and models with works by Ludwig Mies van der Rohe, Mart Stam, and Walter Gropius, Weimar, 1923

selected as authors for the series. Some of them were already linked to the Bauhaus through existing relationships, while some had attracted attention as critics of the Bauhaus, such as De Stijl member Theo van Doesburg.

5. Notable People in the Network and their Work in the Bauhaus Context

Not every artist and author who was asked to contribute to *Neue Europäische Graphik*, the *Internationale Architekturausstellung*, and the *Bauhausbücher* continued to work closely with the Bauhaus beyond these projects. The following section presents individuals (listed in alphabetical order) who contributed to those three projects and, beyond this, also accompanied and helped shape the Bauhaus. They are described in brief, with special regard to their working relationships and without any claim to completeness.

George Antheil
(b. 1900 in Trenton, New Jersey, USA; d. 1959 in New York City, New York, USA)
The "Futurist pianist" was a member of the November Group; 1922 contact with Moholy-Nagy, who inspired him to new forms of musical notation. The Bauhaus member Kurt Schmidt was inspired by Antheil's music in 1923 for the accompaniment to his *Ballet Mécanique*. For the *Bauhausbücher* series, he was asked to write *Musico-Mechanico*. In December 1928, he gave a piano recital at the Bauhaus. Xanti Schawinsky later remarked that pieces by Antheil were also played by the Bauhaus Band.[15]

Willi Baumeister
(b. 1889 in Stuttgart, Germany; d. 1955 in Stuttgart, Germany)
Studied with Adolf Hölzel, where he met Schlemmer. In 1919, together with Schlemmer and others, he founded the artist group *Üecht*. From 1913 onward, contact with the Sturm circle. Contacts to Klee, Fernand Léger, Le Corbusier, and Ozenfant. Represented with a work in the third *Neue Europäische Graphik* portfolio. From 1927 onward, a member of the Circle of New Graphic Designers, the chairman of which was Schwitters. In the same year, collaboration with Mies van der Rohe and Lilly Reich for the exhibition of the Werkbund

(Association of Craftsmen) at the Weissenhof Estate in Stuttgart. Founding of the Frankfurt October Group in 1928 together with Stam and the former Bauhaus member Adolf Meyer; in 1929, Baumeister rejected the offer of Hannes Meyer, with whom he was on friendly terms, to teach at the Bauhaus. From the end of September to the beginning of October 1929, an exhibition of his *Sport and Machine* series was on view at the Bauhaus. In 1929, his article "bildbau" (pictorial composition) appeared in issue no. 4 of the *bauhaus* magazine. Donation of a work for the 1933 Bauhaus carnival lottery in Berlin, which was won by Mies van der Rohe.

Adolf Behne
(b. 1885 in Magdeburg, Germany; d. 1948 in Berlin, Germany)
1914 first meeting with Gropius, with whom he exchanged ideas about the German Werkbund. In 1918, the architect, publicist, and art critic cofounded the Workers Council for Art; in 1919, he became its managing director. That same year, his book *The Return of Art* was published, which, like other of his books, was in the Bauhaus library in Weimar. From then on, he was associated with the Bauhaus as an advocate and constructive critic. Close friendship with Gropius and friendly relations with several masters. May 1920, lecture at the Bauhaus titled "Attempt at a Cosmic View of Art". From 1921 onward, intensive contacts to the De Stijl movement; 1922 publication of the book *Contemporary Dutch Architecture*, numerous articles on the Bauhaus. Contact in 1923 with Karel Teige. Together with Behne, several books were planned for the Russia series of *Bauhausbücher*, as well as *Art, Crafts, and Industry* and, together with Max Burchartz, *The Sculpture of Design*. From around 1927 onward, he exchanged letters with Hannes Meyer. May 1930 lecture titled "Critical Cross-Sectional View of Art" at the Bauhaus.

Peter Behrens
(b. 1868 in Hamburg, Germany; d. 1940 in Berlin, Germany)
From 1908 to 1910, Gropius was employed in the office of the architect and industrial designer Peter Behrens; later, Bauhaus master Adolf Meyer (1907–1908) also worked

11   *A Magyar Mérnök és Építész egylet Közlönye* (Newsletter of the Hungarian Association of Architects and Engineers), Budapest, 25 October 1923; quoted in: Staatliches Bauhaus Weimar (ed.), *Pressestimmen für das Staatliche Bauhaus Weimar, Weimar 1925*, pp. 60f., here p. 60, reprint, ed. Peter Hahn (Munich, 1980) [translated].

12   Siehe Alain Findeli, "László Moholy-Nagy und das Projekt der Bauhausbücher", in: Ute Brüning (ed.), *Das A und O des Bauhauses. Bauhauswerbung, Schriftbilder, Drucksachen, Ausstellungsdesign* (Leipzig, 1995), pp. 22–6.

13   Announcement of the *Bauhausbücher* [1924], in: Brüning 1995 (see note 12), p. 116.

14   See: "Aufruf" 1924 (see note 1), p. 325 [translated].

15   See: Xanti Schawinsky, "metamorphose bauhaus", in: Magdalena Droste and Boris Friedewald (eds.), *Unser Bauhaus. Bauhäusler und Freunde erinnern sich* (Munich/London/New York, 2019), pp. 267–73, here p. 269.

there, as did Mies van der Rohe (1908–1911) and Le Corbusier (1910–1911). In 1923, Behrens was represented at the Bauhaus in the *Internationale Architekturausstellung*. In 1924, he wrote a letter of protest to the Thuringian government against the closure of the Bauhaus. Permanent member of the board of trustees of the Friends of the Bauhaus, founded in 1924 together with Kokoschka and Chagall in order to support the Bauhaus "morally and practically". 1927 buildings for the Weissenhof Estate (general management: Mies van der Rohe).

Marc Chagall
(b. 1887 in Vitebsk, Belarus; d. 1985 in Saint-Paul-de-Vence, France)
1914 first solo exhibition in the gallery Der Sturm. From 1919 onward, in the circle of the November Group. Chagall was represented with a work in the fourth Bauhaus portfolio. Permanent member of the board of trustees of the Friends of the Bauhaus, founded in 1924.

Albert Gleizes
(b. 1881 in Paris, France; d. 1953 in Avignon, France)
The French painter exhibited in the gallery Der Sturm before the First World War. He had promised a work for the "French" Bauhaus portfolio in the *Neue Europäische Graphik* series. In 1928, his book *Cubism* appeared in the *Bauhausbücher* series. In April 1932, he gave a lecture at the Bauhaus titled "The Workshops for Artists and Intellectuals in Moly-Sabata", referring to an artist community he had founded in France in 1927. At the last carnival in February 1933, a work by Gleizes was raffled off.

Le Corbusier
(Charles-Édouard Jeanneret; b. 1887 in La Chaux-de-Fonds, Switzerland; d. 1965 in Roquebrune-Cap-Martin, France)
From 1910 to 1911, the architect and painter worked as a technical draughtsman in Peter Behrens's architectural office in Babelsberg. In 1922, Le Corbusier had promised a work for the "French" Bauhaus portfolio. He was represented with several works in the *Internationale Architekturausstellung*, including a model of his "Living Machine".

In 1923, he met Gropius for the first time in Paris and was to write a book titled *Architecture* for the *Bauhausbücher* series. In 1927, he was represented with two houses in the Weissenhof Estate. Issue no. 4 of the magazine *bauhaus* (1929) included the text "geometrie" from his book *Urban Development*.

Ernst (Ernő) Kállai
(b. 1880 in Săcălaz, Romania; d. 1954 in Budapest, Hungary)
Since 1915, the art critic and journalist published articles on Constructivist art in the journal *MA*, published by Lajos Kassák, under the pseudonym Péter Mátyá. The magazine featured works by Schlemmer, Moholy-Nagy, and Gleizes. In 1922, he belonged to the Constructivist group around the Berlin-based artist Gert Caden with Moholy-Nagy, Ludwig Mies van der Rohe, and Bauhaus member Werner Graeff. In 1923, he signed an art-political manifesto with Moholy-Nagy, among others, which appeared in 1923 in issue no. 4 of the Hungarian magazine *Egység* and which expressed support for a "new communist culture".[16] For the *Bauhausbücher* series, *The Work of the MA Group* was planned, which he was to write together with Kassák. After Hannes Meyer had become director of the Bauhaus, Kállái became secretary of the magazine *bauhaus* in 1928, for which he wrote several articles. In autumn 1929, he left the Bauhaus disappointed.

Oskar Kokoschka
(b. 1886 in Pöchlarn, Austria; d. 1980 in Montreaux, Switzerland)
The painter had worked for the *Sturm* magazine since 1910. His works, which Gropius first saw there in 1912, were presented in the gallery Der Sturm. From 1912 onward, he had a relationship with Alma Mahler, who was already a friend of Gropius at the time and whom she married in 1915. Kokoschka was represented with a work in the fourth Bauhaus portfolio. In 1924, together with "culturally significant individuals from Vienna", he signed a letter to the Thuringian Parliament protesting the closure of the Bauhaus. Permanent member of the board of trustees of the Friends of the Bauhaus, founded in 1924.

Jaromír Krejcar
(b. 1895 in Hundsheim, Austria; d. 1950 in London, Great Britain)
From 1923 onward, together with Karl Teige, among others, publisher of *Disk* in Prague, which saw itself as an international magazine; the first issue featured a text by Mies van der Rohe and a photo by Gropius. The magazine's "Italian correspondent" was the artist Ernesto Prampolini, who was represented in the fourth Bauhaus portfolio. A member of the Czech avant-garde group Devětsil. In 1923, represented with a draft design at the *Internationale Architekturausstellung* at the Bauhaus. From 1929, he brokered and sold Bauhaus products in Prague, including chairs covered with fabric by Bauhaus member Peer Bücking, as reported in 1930 in a special issue of the magazine *ReD*, published in Prague. Encounters with Hannes Meyer in Prague during his Bauhaus years. From 1931 to 1932, the former Bauhaus members Antonín Urban and Peer Bücking worked on the construction of the sanatorium Machnáč in Czechoslovakia (today the Slovak Republic), which he had designed. In 1932, he criticised the architecture of Mies van der Rohe in the Czech magazine *Žijeme*.

Alfred Kubin
(b. 1877 in Litoměřice, Bohemia, today the Czech Republic; d. 1959 in Wernstein am Inn, Austria)
In 1909, together with Kandinsky, the painter was among the founding members of the New Artists' Association in Munich. He was represented in the fifth Bauhaus portfolio. In December 1931, Kubin visited his friend Klee in Dessau; this encounter gave rise to the idea of an exhibition of Kubin's work at the Bauhaus, which was realised in June 1932.

El Lissitzky
(b. 1890 in Pochinok, Russia; d. 1941 in Moscow, Russia)
From 1922 onward, he belonged to the circle of the November Group in Berlin. Gropius apparently wanted to bring him to the Bauhaus as a master in 1923, but finally decided on Moholy-Nagy instead.[17] For the *Bauhausbücher* series, a volume by him on *New Advertising and Typography* was planned. In October 1926, he visited Gropius and the Bauhaus in Dessau. Two years later, he gave the lecture

16   Quoted in: Krisztina Passuth, *Moholy-Nagy* (Weingarten 1986), pp. 307–8, here p. 308 [translated].

17   See: Hubert Hoffmann, "das dessauer und das moskauer Bauhaus (WCHUTEMAS). ihre gegenseitigen beziehungen", in: Droste/Friedewald 2019 (see note 15), pp. 150–3, here p. 151.

18   See: The Museum of Modern Art (ed.), *One and One is Four. The Bauhaus Photocollages of Josef Albers* (New York, 2016), pp. 69f.

19   See: Suzanne Strum, *The Ideal of Total Environmental Control, Knud Lönberg-Holm, Buckminster Fuller, and the SSA* (London/New York, 2018), Kindle version, pp. 10f.

20   Annemarie Jaeggi, *Adolf Meyer. Der zweite Mann. Ein Architekt im Schatten von Walter Gropius* (Berlin, 1994), pp. 152–6.

21   Mienke Simon Thomas, "Netherlands – Bauhaus. Pre-Digital Networks Between 1910 and 1970", in: Museum Boijmans van Beuningen (ed.), *Netherlands – Bauhaus, pioneers of a new world* (Rotterdam, 2019), pp. 10–25, here p. 22.

22   Ibid.

23   The Museum of Modern Art (ed.), *One and One is Four, The Bauhaus Photocollages of Josef Albers* (New York, 2016), p. 73.

24   For more on Schwitters's early connection to the Bauhaus, see: Isabel Schulz, "'Märchen unserer Zeit'. Kurt Schwitters als Vortragskünstler am Bauhaus", in: Peter Bernhard: *bauhausvorträge. Gastredner am Bauhaus 1919–1925* (Berlin, 2017), pp. 299–306.

"Architecture and Workmanship" at the Bauhaus. In June 1930, he visited the Bauhaus once again, where he was photographed by Josef Albers, who arranged the photos into two collages.[18]

Knud Lönberg-Holm
(b. 1895 in Copenhagen, Denmark; d. 1972 in New York City, New York, USA)
In 1922, the Danish architect was in the Constructivist circle around the artist Caden, in Berlin, where he met, among others, El Lissitzky, Moholy-Nagy, Kállai, van Doesburg, Mies van der Rohe, and Graeff. Like Max Taut and Gropius, he was a competitor for the Chicago Tribune Tower. All three designs were shown at the 1923 *Internationale Architekturausstellung* at the Bauhaus. In 1923, he emigrated to the USA and became a point of contact for European architects who travelled to America, such as Erich Mendelsohn. In 1924, at his suggestion, methods of the Bauhaus preliminary course and the Russian art school VChUTEMAS were taught at the University of Michigan.[19] A book by him with the title *On Building* was planned for the *Bauhausbücher* series. Correspondent of the Swiss magazine and group *ABC: Contributions to Building*, for which Hannes Meyer also worked; Meyer was in correspondence with him for many years. From 1929 to 1931, he published numerous articles in *Architectural Record* on European modernism, including articles on Gropius, Mies van der Rohe and the Bauhaus. Visited the Bauhaus in Dessau in 1931.

Erich Mendelsohn
(b. 1887 in Allenstein, German Reich, today Olsztyn, Poland; d. 1953 in San Francisco, California, USA)
Founding member of the November Group, supporter of the Workers Council for Art. Represented with two works at the *Internationale Architekturausstellung* at the Bauhaus in 1923. In March 1928, slide lecture at the Bauhaus "Russia and America: an Architectural Cross Section". In 1930, he commissioned Oskar Schlemmer to create a relief for his private house; the work, however, was never executed. In June 1932, he guided Bauhaus students through his private house in Berlin and showed them the Columbus House he had designed.

Jacobus Johannes Pieter Oud
(b. 1890 in Purmerend, Netherlands; d. 1963 in Wassenaar, Netherlands)
From 1917 to 1921, member of the Dutch De Stijl group. 1921 presumably the first contact with the Bauhaus: meeting with Adolf Meyer, the Bauhaus master for Building Theory and head of Gropius's private building studio, when Oud visited van Doesburg in Weimar. At that time, Oud influenced the architecture of Meyer and Gropius.[20] In conjunction with the Bauhaus exhibition, he gave the lecture "New Building in Holland" in August 1923; represented with several works at the *Internationale Architekturausstellung*. Gropius made him several offers to teach at the Bauhaus.[21] Friendship with Moholy-Nagy. In 1924, he wrote a letter of protest to the Thuringian government and the state parliament against the closure of the Bauhaus. In 1926, his book *Dutch Architecture* was published as part of the *Bauhausbücher*. In 1929, a group of thirty Bauhaus students visited Oud's Van Nelle factory building in Rotterdam.[22]

Amédée Ozenfant
(b. 1886 in Saint-Quentin, France; d. 1966 in Cannes, France)
In 1920, together with Le Corbusier and others, he founded the avant-garde magazine *L´Esprit Nouveau* (The New Spirit), to which the Bauhaus in Weimar had subscribed for its library. One work was intended for the "French" Bauhaus portfolio. Member of the *Cercle et Carré* (Circle and Square) artists' association founded in Paris in 1929, together with, among others, Le Corbusier, Baumeister, Gropius, and Kandinsky. In 1931, his essay "my visit to the textile workshop of the bauhaus" was published in issue no. 2 of the magazine *bauhaus*, after he had visited the Bauhaus in the same year. In the summer of 1931, Albers photographed him and made a photo-collage from the pictures.[23] Between 1931 and 1932, the former Bauhaus member Gotthardt Itting studied painting with Ozenfant in Paris.

Kurt Schwitters
(b. 1887 in Hanover, Germany; d. 1948 in Kendal, Great Britain)
In 1918, first contacts to the Sturm movement; first contact to the Bauhaus via Behne.[24]

Represented with a work in the third Bauhaus portfolio in 1922. That same year, participation in the conference of the Constructivist International Creative Association in Weimar together with the Dadaists Arp and Tzara and the Constructivists El Lissitzky, van Doesburg, and Graeff, as well as Moholy-Nagy, with whom he was friendly during this time. In January 1925, reading from his *Fairytales of Our Time* at the Bauhaus in Weimar, presumably including parts of the *Ursonate*. In his narrative prose, member of the Bauhaus also appeared, among them "Uncle Gropius" and "Uncle Moholy".[25] A *Merz* book by Schwitters was planned for the *Bauhausbücher* series. April 1926 lecture at the Bauhaus in Dessau, participation in the opening of the Bauhaus building. In 1928, founding of the Ring of German Graphic Designers, together with, among others, Max Burchartz, Willi Baumeister, and Moholy-Nagy. He presumably visited the Bauhaus between 1927 and 1929.[26]

Mart Stam
(b. 1899 in Purmerend, Netherlands; d. 1986 in Goldach, Switzerland)
Participation with a draft design at the *Internationale Architekturausstellung* in Weimar in 1923. Cofounder of the Swiss magazine and group *ABC: Contributions to Building*, first published in 1924, on which Lissitzky and Hannes Meyer also cooperated. An *ABC of Building* was planned for the *Bauhausbücher* series. In 1926, Gropius offered him the position of Head of the Building Department at the Bauhaus in Dessau, but Stam refused. In 1927, cofounder of the Frankfurt October Group together with, among others, Willi Baumeister and Adolf Meyer. 1927 terraced house for the Weissenhof Estate. From 1928 to 1929, guest lecturer for Urban Planning and the Theory of Building at the Bauhaus. In June 1928, he gave a lecture on "M-Art" at the Bauhaus and participated as a representative of the Netherlands in the first CIAM conference in La Sarraz, Switzerland, in which Hannes Meyer also participated.

Karel Teige
(b. 1900 in Prague, Czech Lands, today Czech Republic; d. 1951 in Prague, Czechoslovakia, today Czech Republic)
In 1920, the painter, publicist, typographer, and Constructivist book artist was a cofounder and head of the Czech avant-garde association Devětsil, to which Krejcar also belonged. From 1923 onward, he was director of the architectural journal *Stavba*; in issue no. 2 (1923), he wrote a critical article about the Bauhaus's tendencies towards the arts and crafts. From 1923 onward, he was also publisher of the international magazine *Disk* in Prague, together with Krejcar, among others. The first issue contained a text by Mies van der Rohe and a photograph of the Chicago Tribune Tower model by Gropius. For the *Bauhausbücher* series, he was to write a volume titled *Czech Art*. From 1928 onward, contact and exchange with Hannes Meyer. As a "Guest Lecturer for Literature", he gave three lectures at the Bauhaus in January 1930 called "Introduction to the Development of the Problematics of Materials and Expression in Contemporary Literature and Poetry".[27] In March 1930, he gave lectures on the theme of "Sociology of the City and Living".[28] In 1930, Meyer wanted to secure him as a permanent employee in the fields of propaganda, writing, stage, and typography.[29] In 1930, together with Hannes Meyer, he edited a special issue of the Czech avant-garde magazine *ReD* on the Bauhaus.

25   See: Gerhard Schaub, "Neun ungedruckte Briefe und Postkarten von Kurt Schwitters an Walter Gropius", in: idem. (ed.), *Kurt Schwitters: "Bürger und Idiot". Beiträge zu Werk und Wirkung eines Gesamtkünstlers* (Berlin, 1993), pp. 141–53, here pp. 145f.

26   Ibid.

27   Hannes Meyer in a letter to Karel Teige, dated 18 December 1929; quoted in: Peter Bernhard, "Meyers Programm der Gastvorträge", in: Philipp Oswalt, *Hannes Meyers neue Baulehre. Von Dessau bis Mexico* (Basel, 2019), pp. 308–15, here p. 311.

28   Jeanette Fabian, "Der tschechische Funktionalismus", in: Thomas Flierl and Philipp Oswalt (eds.), *Hannes Meyer und das Bauhaus. Im Streit der Deutungen* (Leipzig, 2018), pp. 329–37, here p. 333.

29   Simone Hain, "Karel Teige: Typografie, Propaganda, Poesie, Architektur", in: Oswalt 2019 (see note 23), pp. 349–92, here p. 362, note 6.

WEIMAR, DESSAU, BERLIN
Boris Friedewald

THE TOTAL WORK OF ART

THE TOTAL WORK OF ART

Staatliche Bildstelle Berlin (Carl Rogge), Haus Sommerfeld in Berlin-Dahlem, view of the courtyard, Walter Gropius und Adolf Meyer (architecture), 1920–1921

In the 1921 Weimar Bauhaus programme, Walter Gropius announced the creation of a *Gesamtkunstwerk*, or total work of art: "The Bauhaus strives for unity in all artistic creation, the reunification of all the disciplines—sculpture, painting, the crafts and trades—to form a new art of building in which they are all indispensable components. The final, if distant, goal of the Bauhaus is the unified work of art—the grand building—in which there are no borders between monumental and decorative art. […] The Bauhaus wishes to train architects, painters, and sculptors of all standards, according to their abilities, to become either hard-working artisans or free artists, and to found a working community of leading and young working artists, a community that knows how to design buildings in their totality—shell construction, fitting out, and ornament and decoration—in a like-minded spirit and unified design."

This "grand building", based on ideals of medieval cathedral construction, remained utopian, but in several projects the Bauhaus did come close to the total work of art. In 1921, students took part in building Walter Gropius and Adolf Meyer's *Haus Sommerfeld* in Berlin. In 1923, numerous masters and students—from the weaving, carpentry, metal, and ceramics workshops—worked on the experimental *Haus Am Horn*, designed by painter and Bauhaus master Georg Muche. The Bauhaus building in Dessau, designed by Walter Gropius and opened in 1926, and the masters' houses there were also "total" works, in which masters and students worked together and used products from the Bauhaus workshops. This led to the making of metal and wooden furniture, lamps, and also to colour plans for the interior.

The wish to create a total work of art is also seen in the work of the theatre workshop, in the expressionist plays of Lothar Schreyer at the Weimar Bauhaus, in which language, gesture, colour, and sculpture were all radically interlinked. Plans for theatre pieces by László Moholy-Nagy, such as the *Sketch of a Score for a Mechanical Eccentricity: Synthesis of Form, Movement, Sound, Light (Colour), and Smell*, also had the character of a total work of art, or a "total work," as Moholy-Nagy put it.

Staatliche Bildstelle Berlin, Haus Am Horn, living room, Marcel Breuer (furniture), Gyula Pap (lamp), Martha Erps (carpet), László Moholy-Nagy (wall light), 1923

Walter Gropius (author), Lyonel Feininger (illustration), Manifesto and programme of the State Bauhaus Weimar, with "Cathedral" cover, April 1920

Aerial view, Bauhaus building Dessau, 1926/1927, 1927

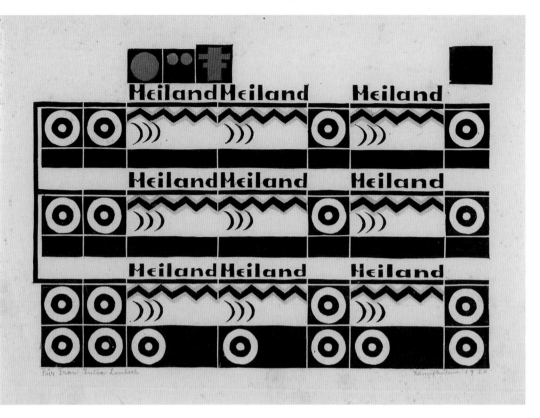

Lothar Schreyer, *Heiland, Heiland*, from the publication *crossplay*, 1920

Herbert Bayer, Emergency currency of the State of Thuringia, 19⋮

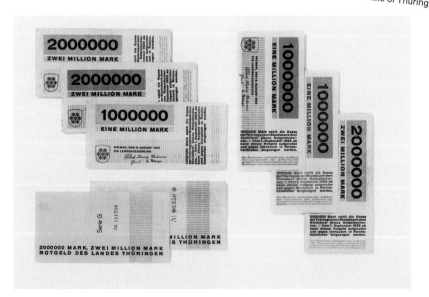

ART CRAFTS TECHNOLOGY

"Architects, sculptors, painters, we all must return to the crafts!" Walter Gropius demanded in the Bauhaus Manifesto of 1919. Therefore, the first goal was to have every student learn a craft in one of the workshops. Artistic creation was only possible on the basis of a handicraft, and the artist was a more intensive kind of artisan.

In early 1922, there was a debate about individual or mass production. Walter Gropius noted: "Master Itten recently demanded that we must decide whether to create individual and unique works in complete contrast to economic realities, or whether we need to get closer to industry." In this debate, Itten himself came down in favour of the individually made unique work, quite in line with the original Bauhaus idea.

Otto Lindig, Dornburg ceramics workshop, Plate, 1922/1923

Gropius announced a decisive new direction in 1923, with the new slogan "Art and Technology—a New Unity". This was to be highly significant for the future development of the Bauhaus, and it led to Johannes Itten's departure from the Bauhaus. In the catalogue of the large Bauhaus Exhibition of 1923 in Weimar, Gropius stated that the Bauhaus was not a school for handicrafts, and that its goal was to create contacts with industry. The workshops would now focus on standardised procedures, making prototypes and models that were suited to industrial serial production. The first results of this new approach were functional products consisting of just a few parts and often very basic shapes, such as the combination teapot by Theodor Bogler, the *Slatted Chair* by Marcel Breuer, the legendary *Bauhaus Lamp* by Carl Jakob Jucker and Wilhelm Wagenfeld, and the Bauhaus chess set by Josef Hartwig.

In 1925, Bauhaus Book No. 7 was published, entitled *New Works from the Bauhaus Workshops*. It amounted to a sales catalogue for Bauhaus products, as Gropius said: "The Bauhaus workshops are primarily laboratories in which models are developed and continually improved for typical products of our time to be produced in series." In the same year, the Bauhaus Dessau published the *Catalogue of Patterns*, in which Bauhaus products were advertised and could be ordered. Gropius had suggested that the main principle in the design of these products was "research into their essence". He said: "A thing is determined by its essence. To be able to design it to work properly—be it a container, a chair, or a house—it is necessary to research its essence first; it should serve its purpose perfectly, being practical and functional, long-lasting, inexpensive, and 'beautiful'."

The Bauhaus was able to derive income from the sale of goods and thereby to gain some independence from the need for public subsidies. Students also benefited, as they participated in the profits from their designs and related licensing, thereby covering part of their living costs. When the Bauhaus moved to the new building in Dessau in 1926, the workshops were equipped with new machines that made it possible to produce prototypes for industry as well as the Bauhaus's own products in larger numbers. This transformed the workshops into real production facilities, where teaching nonetheless continued.

It was under the charge of Hannes Meyer, who advocated "the needs of the people before the needs of luxury", that the most successful standard Bauhaus product was made. These were the Bauhaus wallpapers, whose designs were chosen in a student competition.

Unknown designer, Structured cloth pattern "Semmering" no. 187, from a pattern book with Bauhaus textiles, 1928–1931

Marianne Brandt, Ashtray, 1924

A
R
T

C
R
A
F
T
S

T
E
C
H
N
O
L
O
G
Y

Unknown designer, Walter Gropius, Houses,
from the publication *State Bauhaus Weimar 1919–1923, 1923*

Firma Rasch, Bauhaus wallpaper patterns, designed by
Bauhaus students

Josef Hartwig (game design), Joost Schmidt (packaging typography),
The Bauhaus chess set, model XVI, 1924

RADICAL PEDAGOGY

Unknown photographer, Wall-painting class in the Bauhaus building, Dessau, 1928/1929

R A D I C A L   P E D A G O G Y

Today the Bauhaus is seen as one of the most innovative and influential art schools of the twentieth century. Walter Gropius, its founder, was certain that "art cannot be controlled, but the technical means can be." This was why the Bauhaus established workshops for wall painting, metals, weaving, and carpentry as the centrepieces in the training of apprentices and journeymen, marking a clear innovation when compared to the classical art academies. The first workshops were the gold, silver, and copper workshop (later the metal workshop), the graphic printing workshop, the bookbinding workshop, and the weaving workshop.
In 1920, there followed the workshops for ceramics, glass painting, wall painting, and wood and stone sculpture. In 1921 the carpentry and theatre workshops were founded.

There were difficulties at first in finding teachers who were able both to teach the appropriate skills and crafts and also address artistic issues. "First, a new generation which was able to combine both qualities had to be educated", Gropius later said. This was the reason that the workshops were jointly led by a "work master", responsible for the practical skills, and a "form master", responsible for formal and design questions. This principle was maintained until the Bauhaus moved to Dessau, when it was dropped.

If students wished to train in one of the workshops, they first had to pass the preliminary course, which was taught by Johannes Itten and later by László Moholy-Nagy and Josef Albers. The preliminary course was intended to develop students' creative abilities, and to free their minds from conventional approaches and the principles of existing and past styles and movements. Gropius said: "First the whole person, and then—as late as possible—specialisation."

Architect Hannes Meyer became Bauhaus director in 1928, and he reorganised the curriculum, merged several workshops, increased the period of study, brought numerous guest teachers in, and also organised lectures by scientists. Meyer consolidated the training of architects, which had only been introduced to the Bauhaus in 1927. He also introduced the teaching of sports and photography. He wanted to focus more than previously on "studies in practice", in particular through participation in joint construction projects, for which very precise analysis of the future uses of the buildings would provide a "scientifically founded design".

When Ludwig Mies van der Rohe was appointed Bauhaus director in 1930, students with the right prior experience and training were able to enrol without having to do the hitherto obligatory preliminary course. A lot of theory was now taught, and the length of studies was significantly cut. In 1930, on the occasion of his appointment, Mies said: "I don't want marmalade, I don't want workshops and school, I want school."

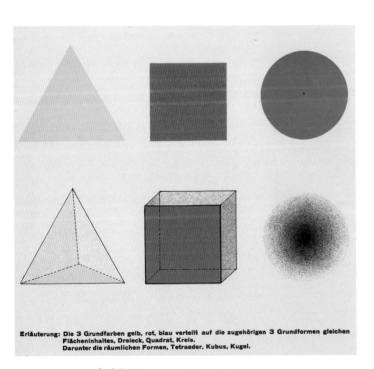

Erläuterung: Die 3 Grundfarben gelb, rot, blau verteilt auf die zugehörigen 3 Grundformen gleichen Flächeninhaltes, Dreieck, Quadrat, Kreis.
Darunter die räumlichen Formen, Tetraeder, Kubus, Kugel.

Ludwig Hirschfeld-Mack, "The three primary colours, yellow, red, blue, distributed on the corresponding primary shapes with identical surface areas, triangle, square, circle …," colour panel from the colours seminar with Ludwig Hirschfeld-Mack, from the publication *State Bauhaus Weimar 1919–1923, 1923*

**R
A
D
I
C
A
L

P
E
D
A
G
O
G
Y**

R
A
D
I
C
A
L

P
E
D
A
G
O
G
Y

Marianne Ahlfeld-Heymann
(attributed), Exercise from
the class Pictorial Form Theory
taught by Paul Klee, 1923–1924

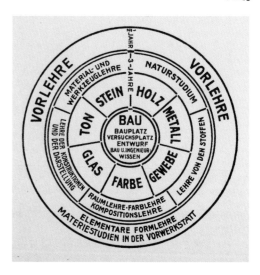

Unknown designer, Scheme of teaching,
from the publication *State Bauhaus Weimar 1919–1923, 1923*

Marianne Ahlfeld-Heymann (attributed),
Exercise from the class Pictorial Form Theory taught by Paul Klee, 1923–1924

COMMUNITY

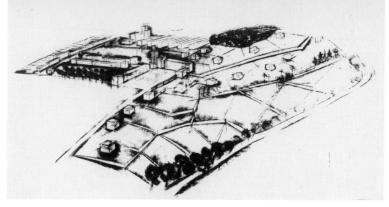

Unknown photographer, Bauhaus living estate area,
Walter Gropius (design), Farkas Mólnar (drawing), 1922

From the very early days, the idea of a
Bauhaus "community" was common currency,
and its meaning shifted in many ways over
the years. In the very first school programme
of April 1919, Walter Gropius emphasised
that the aim was "to train architects, painters,
and sculptors of all standards, according to
their abilities, to become either hard-working
artisans or free artists, and to found a
working community of leading and young
working artists."

As well as this working community, Gropius
was just as interested in the living community
of masters and students, which he also
noted expressly in the Bauhaus programme.
This was a community with shared leisure
activities, particularly evident in the Bauhaus
evening events and the legendary Bauhaus
parties. In 1932, Bauhaus director Ludwig
Mies van der Rohe also noted the importance of this working and living community,
just as the closure of the Dessau Bauhaus
was imminent: "There is no educational
institution to match the Bauhaus in Germany
and the whole world. Particularly in the past
two years, relations between teachers and
students in Dessau have gained a far greater
quality of cooperation than can be achieved
in any other German university." And van der
Rohe's predecessor, Hannes Meyer, also
made the cooperative and collective work of
everyone at the Bauhaus his guiding principle.

Hannes Meyer (publisher), Ernst Kállai (editor),
bauhaus. journal for design 2/3, 1928

The goal of a cohesive community at the Bauhaus was, however, repeatedly challenged by the formation of specific interest groups, such as the separatist Mazdaznan community led by Johannes Itten at the early Bauhaus, and also by communist groups during the eras of Hannes Meyer and Mies van der Rohe. And the "equality of the sexes" that Gropius had proclaimed at the beginning was not always easy—it had to be renegotiated in the Bauhaus community many times over the years.

Kurt Kranz, Iwao and Michiko Yamawaki on the terrace of the Bauhaus canteen in Dessau, 1927

from left: Marta Erps-Breuer, Katt Both, Ruth Hollos-Consemüller, 1927
Erich Consemüller, Marcel Breuer and his "harem",

alle kreise der kulturwelt

Bauhaus Dessau, Advertising brochure / order card for the journal *bauhaus, all the circles of the cultural world*, folder, 1927

Unknown photographer, Montage with photos of the student demonstration to protest the dismissal of Bauhaus director Hannes Meyer, 1930

C
O
M
M
U
N
I
T
Y

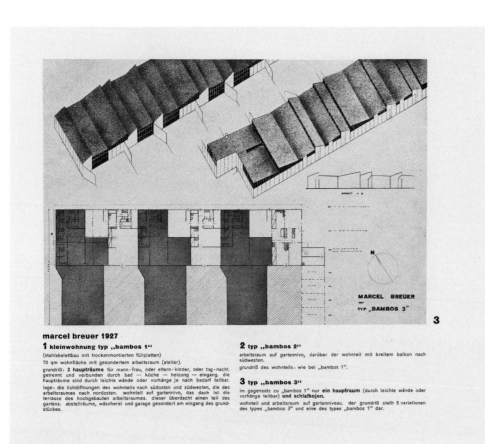

marcel breuer 1927

1 kleinwohnung typ „bambos 1"
(stahlskelettbau mit trockenmontierten füliplatten).
70 qm wohnfläche mit gesondertem arbeitsraum (atelier).
grundriß: **2 haupträume** für mann-frau, oder eltern-kinder, oder tag-nacht.
getrennt und verbunden durch bad — küche — heizung — eingang. die
haupträume sind durch leichte wände oder vorhänge je nach bedarf teilbar.
lage: die lichtöffnungen des wohnteils nach südosten und südwesten, die des
arbeitsraumes nach nordosten. wohnteil auf gartennivo, das dach ist die
terrasse des hochgebauten arbeitsraumes. dieser überdacht einen teil des
gartens. abstellräume, wäscherei und garage gesondert am eingang des grund-
stückes.

2 typ „bambos 2"
arbeitsraum auf gartennivo, darüber der wohnteil mit breitem balkon nach
südwesten.
grundriß des wohnteils: wie bei „bambos 1".

3 typ „bambos 3"
im gegensatz zu „bambos 1" nur **ein hauptraum** (durch leichte wände oder
vorhänge teilbar) **und schlafkojen.**
wohnteil und arbeitsraum auf gartenniveau. der grundriß stellt 5 variationen
des types „bambos 3" und eine des types „bambos 1" dar.

Marcel Breuer, *Bambos 3*,
design for a settlement in
Dessau for young masters, from
bauhaus. journal for design
1, 1928

Lotte Gerson-Collein, The largest and the smallest Bauhaus
members, Peter Bücking and Takehiko Mizutani in the vestibule
of the Bauhaus building in Dessau, from *bauhaus. journal for desi*
2/3, 1928

Edmund Collein, Members of the Bauhaus on a swimming trip to the Elbe, 1928

FLOATING

T. Lux Feininger, Eurythmics, 1927

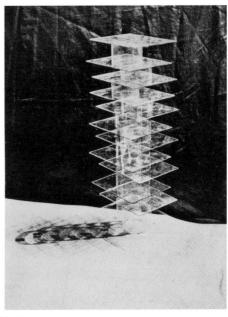

Edmund Collein, Construction model made of glass, preliminary course with Josef Albers, 1927/1928

FLOATING

The themes of suspension and floating featured at the Bauhaus in various guises— as motifs in architecture and fine art, and as metaphors for a modern way of life. In 1926, Marcel Breuer demonstrated the design of his chairs in his collage, *A Bauhaus Film*, beginning with the *African Chair*, made at the Bauhaus in 1921. The series of designs culminated in a vision of a seated person floating on an "elastic column of air"—Breuer left the actual date when this might become reality open. Furniture made of steel tubing, like Breuer's and Ludwig Mies van der Rohe's cantilever chairs, also demonstrate this desire to overcome material restrictions.

After the Bauhaus reopened in Dessau in 1926, students and masters began to take photographs that either showed floating people or objects, or presented them as if they were about to take off. Paul Klee had already addressed this theme back in 1923, in his lithograph *The Tightrope Walker*. The figure of the tightrope walker stands for a futuristic, modern type of man, whose longing to escape gravity takes him into heady heights, and who yet still needs a rope under his feet and a pole for balance.

Mies van der Rohe's design for a *Skyscraper in Glass and Reinforced Concrete* also negated all sense of weight, and the transparency of the construction gave the impression that it was about to dissolve. The same effect is true of the Dessau Bauhaus building designed by Walter Gropius, particularly when it is lit up at night. In 1923, Gropius noted: "The increasing stability and greater mass of modern building materials (iron, concrete, glass) and the increasing boldness of new suspended constructions mean that the sense of gravity that pertained to older ways of building is now being transformed." In the Dessau Bauhaus building, there were always a number of "suspended sculptures" on show, made by students in Moholy-Nagy's preliminary course, which the teacher saw as valuable preliminaries toward "a highly spiritual form," and specifically "kinetic sculptures."

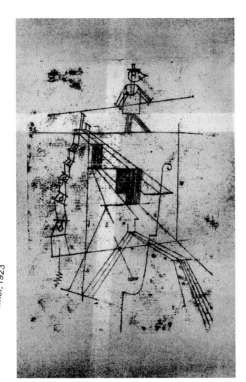

Paul Klee, *Tightrope Walker*, 1923

Leo Baron, Gertrud Herold on the roof of the Bauhaus building in Dessau, 1929

F
L
O
A
T
I
N
G

Kurt Schmidt, Construction for fireworks, from the Stage Workshop, 1923

Ludwig Mies van der Rohe, Armchair MR 534, 1927–1932

FLOATING

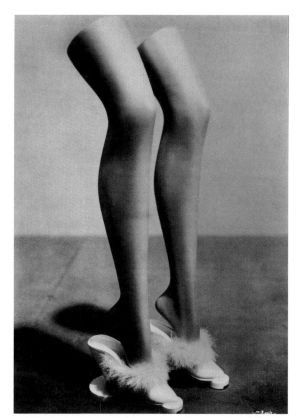

Umbo (Otto Umbehr), Slippers, 1926

ENCOUNTERS

Walter Gropius, László Moholy-Nagy (editors), *International Architecture*, Bauhaus books no. 1, 1925

E
N
C
O
U
N
T
E
R
S

From the very beginning, the Bauhaus wanted its work to be seen outside Germany, not least in order to attract students from all over the world. With this in mind, Walter Gropius wrote letters in 1920 to Japan, Mexico, Turkey, Brazil, Peru, and Chile, praising the fact that the Bauhaus was known "beyond Germany's borders" and that its "many artists from many countries […] had international renown." Gropius's endeavours were continued by his successor, Swiss architect Hannes Meyer, who, writing in several languages in the Bauhaus's own magazine, invited prospective students to come to the Bauhaus. In 1929, there were 140 German students and 30 foreigners, from Poland, Russia, Lithuania, the Netherlands, the USA, Palestine, Turkey, Persia, and Japan. The textile artist Gunta Stölzl later wrote: "The international student body promoted cooperative learning amongst comrades." Some of these students were to take the Bauhaus idea around the world, participating in international architecture competitions and founding their own institutes. Examples include the Hungarian Sándor Bortnyk, who established the "Mühely"—the "little Bauhaus"— in 1928 in Budapest, and Renshichirō Kawakita, cofounder in 1932 of the Japanese "Institute for Life Design."

Bauhaus products also found their way around the world right from the start. In 1922, there were vendors in Vienna, Amsterdam, Leicester, and the USA offering items from the Bauhaus workshops. The Bauhaus also showed its work in exhibitions all over the world, including a 1922 presentation in Calcutta with pictures by masters and students, shown together with contemporary Indian painters. In 1929, there was a touring exhibition of Bauhaus work, shown in Basel, Zurich, Breslau, and other cities. In the same year, works from the Bauhaus workshops were shown at the World's Fair in Barcelona, and in 1930 there was a touring exhibition in the USA (in Cambridge and New York). In 1931, Hannes Meyer presented the first Bauhaus Exhibition in Moscow, which focused on the years 1928–1930, when he had been director.

Many international artists and intellectuals also visited the Bauhaus, among them Solomon Guggenheim and Marcel Duchamp. Some guests came to give lectures or teach, like the composers Béla Bartók and Henry Cowell, Sufi master Murschid Inayat Khan, or Naum Gabo and El Lissitzky. As these visits demonstrate, the Bauhaus was open to the world, with a cross-cultural awareness that shaped teaching and the workshops, and which was not restricted to a "cult of India" and "Americanism", as Oskar Schlemmer noted in 1921.

In the Bauhaus Books published between 1925 and 1930, the Bauhaus was not only able to secure international artists and architects as authors; these books also showcased the Bauhaus as a focal point for the leaders of the avant-garde, as clearly seen in the 1923 portfolio *New European Prints, 4th Portfolio—Italian and Russian Artists* and in the *Exhibition of International Architects* that was part of the Bauhaus Exhibition in the same year. When he became Bauhaus director in Dessau, Mies van der Rohe wrote a letter to America trying to acquire "international" partner institutes with which the Bauhaus could cooperate across borders.

imdu babauhaus!
venez étudier à bauhaus!
studiato nel bauhaus!
come and study at the bauhaus!
tanuljatok a bauhausnál!
studjnjcie w bauhausie!
studujete v bauhausu!
studiert am bauhaus!

Hannes Meyer (editor), "study at the bauhaus!" *bauhaus. journal for design* 2/3, 1928

Iwao Yamawaki, Article on the photocollages of Kurt Kranz, *KOGA* no. 12, vol. 2, 1933

ENCOUNTERS

Unknown photographer, Bauhaus members visiting VKhUTEMAS in Moscow with Peter Bücking, Gunta Stölzl, Arkadij Mordwinow, and Arieh Sharon, third from the right in back, 12 May 1928

Alfred Bischoff, Pi-o-Murshid Hazrat Inayat Khan in Jena, 1921

Unknown photographer, Barbara Josephine Guggenheim, Wassily Kandinsky, Hilla von Rebay, and Solomon R. Guggenheim in the garden of the Dessau masters' houses settlement, 1929

E
N
C
O
U
N
T
E
R
S

THE NEW MAN

It was the atmosphere of new beginnings, particularly after the First World War, that people at the Bauhaus embraced from the outset, and that particularly attracted the young. They not only wanted to give a new shape to the world tomorrow, but also to their own lives. Bauhaus members quickly gained a reputation for unconventionality, which included their bob hairstyles and the relaxed relations between men and women, and also the fact that some Bauhaus families were living together without being married.

THE NEW MAN

As early as May 1919, when the Bauhaus had only been open for just a few weeks, painter and Bauhaus master Lyonel Feininger wrote to his wife, Julia: "What I have seen from the students thus far looks very self-assured. Nearly all of them were soldiers during the war. This is a completely new kind of person. I think they all want to create something new in art and are no longer so timid and harmless." And in 1921 Oskar Schlemmer declared "that the Bauhaus is 'building' in a very different sense than expected—building people. Gropius seems to be very aware of this, and he notes the weaknesses of the academies here, where educating people to be people is neglected." But what this new person might actually look like, and which values and capabilities he or she would have, was a subject of controversy throughout the entire Bauhaus period. Johannes Itten, for example, thought that breathing and physical exercises and a vegetarian diet must promote individual self-awareness, while Oskar Schlemmer focused on theatre, in which the relationship of every character to space was to be explored beyond the level of a "typical body". There was also painting and photography, where abstraction, distortion, and collage were leading to new images of humanity, and the "communist faction" of students in favour of a "world revolution" under director Hannes Meyer, who saw himself as a "scientific Marxist".

Richard Oelze, *Self-Portrait with Girlfriend*, 1922/1923

The goal of work at the Bauhaus was to make contemporary products for a new and future generation. For art critic Adolf Behne, this was evident in the architecture of Walter Gropius's Bauhaus building: "Here in the new Dessau Bauhaus building we see a striking and pure expression […] of the fact that a new type of man and a new relationship to the world is both the starting point and the aim of this new movement in architecture. New materials, new forms of construction, and new technologies are important and must be discussed, tried out, and observed. But they are only a means to an end, and the highest end is man himself."

Fritz Kuhr, *Self-Portrait*, 1927

Oskar Schlemmer, Schematic overview of teaching in the subject "Man", from *bauhaus. journal for design* 2/3, 1928

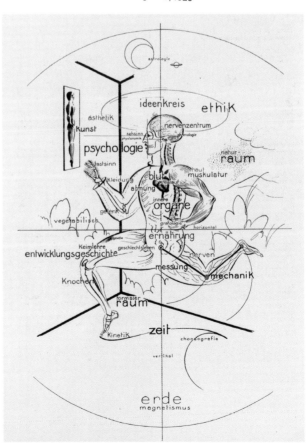

O. Z. Hanish, David Ammann, "Masdasnan – Breathing Lessons", 1919

THE NEW MAN

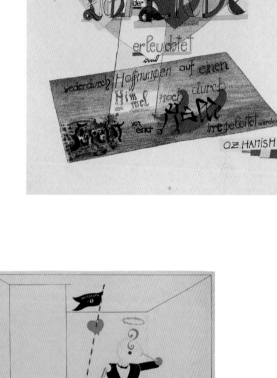

T H E N E W M A N

Oskar Schlemmer, Seated figure, Figure "S", 1921

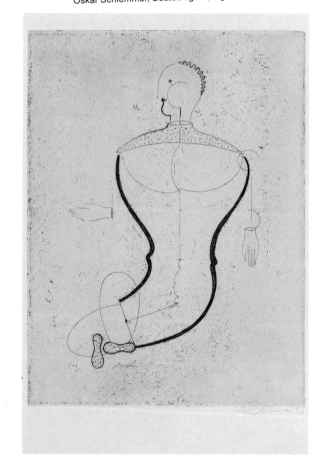

Herbert Bayer, *The Model Bauhaus Man*, 1923

EXPERIMENT

From the moment it was founded, the Bauhaus masters and students were criticised for their focus on mere experimentation—especially by conservatives in government and society. The whole Bauhaus was just one big experiment, they said. While these critics wished to discredit the Bauhaus, experimentation was in fact a very deliberate and significant principle at the Bauhaus, where it went far beyond teaching and theory. Members of the Bauhaus were very sure that the new approaches that they were keenly seeking after the Great War could only be explored in a spirit of experimentation. This was not meant as scientific experiment, but as a free and playful testing of ideas, as all the students in the preliminary course were to discover. But because experimentation frequently led to very practical problems in the teaching of specific skills in the workshops, in late 1921 Gropius planned a specific space dedicated to experimenting, "since, as a practical matter, it is very difficult to unite purely experimental work and the implementation of real works in one and the same workshop."

At the Bauhaus Exhibition in 1923, the institution presented its experiments through a diverse overview, including an "experimental house" they built as a technological, ecological, and living experiment all at the same time; also presented was the *Reflecting Colour-Light-Play* by the students Ludwig Hirschfeld-Mack and Kurt Schwerdtfeger.

When the Bauhaus moved to Dessau in 1925, the workshops were renamed "laboratory workshops", and the use of all lowercase letters was introduced in correspondence, brochures, and the Bauhaus's own magazine—a decision which was heavily criticised in bourgeois circles. This gave Gropius good reason to note again the principally experimental character of the Bauhaus: "the Bauhaus is primarily an experimental institute for the whole country, in all fields of design. it is also not only our right but certainly our duty to continue to test things that have not yet been tested."

In Dessau, Marcel Breuer experimented with furniture made of curved steel piping, while Oskar Schlemmer finally had a dedicated "experimental theatre" in the Bauhaus building. Then there was photography—in no other field was there so much experimentation outside of class than with the camera and film developing techniques, particularly thanks to the use of the compact camera. Werner David Feist, who began his studies at the Bauhaus in 1927, looked back: "Experimenting, testing the limits, breaking rules and regulations, discovering new fields—this was the overarching spirit at the Bauhaus."

Lisbeth Oestreicher, Pattern for curtain material, 1930

Grete Reichardt (attributed), Weaving sample, 1926–1931

E
X
P
E
R
I
M
E
N
T

EXPERIMENT

Marcel Breuer, *Chair B5*, 1926

Hubert Hoffmann, *Boltless Shelf*, dismountable book shelf, prototype, detail, 1930

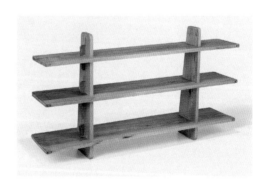

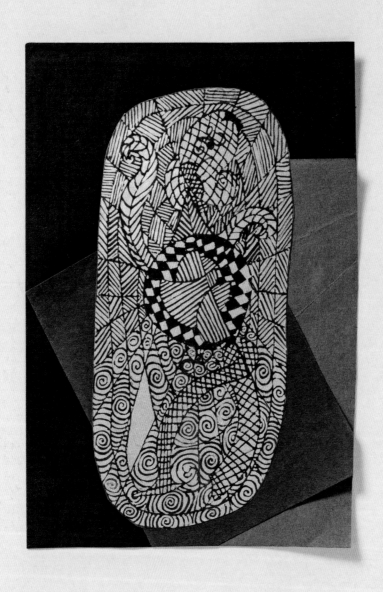

Lena Meyer-Bergner
Untitled, collage of several pieces of coloured paper,
ink pen drawing, partly coloured, 1946–1949
Collection of Gerald Fingerle

In 1939, Lena Meyer-Bergner and her husband, former Bauhaus director Hannes Meyer, moved to Mexico City, where the couple lived until 1949. After training in the weaving workshop at the Bauhaus, Lena Bergner followed Meyer to Moscow, where they married in 1931. Meyer bought the book *Paul Klee* in Mexico City in 1946, when it appeared in its third edition, published by Margaret Miller for the Museum of Modern Art in New York. A stamp shows that he acquired it at the Central Bookshop, while the handwritten signature indicates in turn that he gave it to his wife as a present. Her collage on the inside front flap of the book is probably an expression of the strong sense of solidarity and reverence she had for Klee, who had taught her form theory in the Bauhaus weaving workshop. The three coloured papers, onto which she glued a white, oval cut-out, have a constructivist effect. Over them is a complex network of lines with hatching running in different directions, creating diamond and spiral patterns. Only by looking more closely can one discern in this network of lines the head of a snake—in the upper area—and then its body, winding right across the flap. One can also see a coiled-up snake in the circle at the centre. We know that during his time in Mexico Meyer took photographs of Mayan and Aztec pyramid sites in Chichén Itzá and Teotihuacán. A snake deity was known to feature not only in these two ancient cultures but also in the religion of the indigenous Otomi community, for whom Meyer-Bergner designed a teaching programme for a weaving school while she was in Mexico, although the plan did not come to fruition. In this work, Meyer-Bergner combines the world of the Bauhaus and European modernism with the world of indigenous communities.

Boris Friedewald

The Whole World a Bauhaus?
The Beginnings of "Internationality" at the Bauhaus
Christoph Wagner

I.

No other art academy of the twentieth century has experienced an international reception to match that of the Bauhaus. In the centenary year of the school's founding, this is decisively confirmed by an international series of events honouring its achievements, from Mexico and the USA to Israel and India. In any enquiry into the foundations of this success, we quickly encounter (hi)stories that have been validated for many years, but which have re-emerged with particular intensity during this centenary: foremost among them, the proposition that the Bauhaus is the most internationally successful art academy of the twentieth century, and—with its combination of art and crafts, white walls and right angles, functionalism and modular construction, glass and concrete, minimalist tubular steel furniture and design icons—created a completely new attitude to life. And, since many Bauhaus students and teachers fled Germany to escape the Nazis, its ideas were exported to every corner of the globe. The whole world a Bauhaus?[1] Art history, too, is sustained—if not surrounded—by such narratives at every turn. One might see this thesis as validated by the international success story of a modernism that has endured up to the present day—with much of its foundation laid in the Bauhaus—but which in the meantime has met with criticism in some quarters. Should the Bauhaus as an "export" not also be read as part of, or even instrumental in, the history of European, and specifically German, economic colonisation? In this respect, has the "unity of art and technology" propagated at the Bauhaus since 1923 not been systemically contaminated by Western-style industrialisation? By what right—one might ask from a postcolonial perspective—do the representatives of the Western canon purveying the "Bauhaus brand" bestow upon the rest of the world the norms and ideals of a "Bauhaus culture"? This is a culture, moreover, whose commercial derivatives have developed over the years under the auspices of globalisation, a phenomenon viewed negatively because it is not structured around peer-level exchange.

And in this process of internationalisation, can the Bauhaus really only be defined as a transmitter, a "broadcaster of high culture" so to speak, or might not the reverse also hold true, based on a new awareness of how one's own identity is determined by international networks? The whole Bauhaus a world? These are some of the questions that should be re-examined, especially in reference to the early years in Weimar when the Bauhaus was founded—a phase that is commonly regarded as "romantic expressive" and that art historians are quick to distinguish from the "international Bauhaus" of the Dessau and Berlin years. For in the founding of the Bauhaus, we can find the nucleus of an internationality, as will be shown through a number of case studies. From today's perspective, this internationality could be criticised to some extent as artistically naïve, as a form of "soft exoticism", or sometimes even as inappropriate, but it is nevertheless part of the history of the Bauhaus and its relationship with the "whole world".

II.

For decades, the image of the institution put forth by Walter Gropius and his artist colleagues was one that promoted the Bauhaus as an art school unshakably based on rationalism and functionality: nowhere, it would seem, was Louis Sullivan's motto "form follows function" manifested more rigorously and pragmatically than at the Bauhaus.[2] In recent years, extensive new research has fundamentally changed this image of the rational Bauhaus.[3] The *African Chair,* discovered in 2004, which Marcel Breuer created in 1921 in collaboration with Gunta Stölzl, is a prime example, with its exotic "African"-looking fabric marking a sharp contrast to the plain tubular steel furniture that was later created at the Bauhaus.[4] It is possible that this African chair, whose function and symbolism are still mysterious today, originally carried an ideological and symbolic charge, in that it was intended as a kind of throne for Bauhaus director Walter Gropius, being the master of an architectural lodge, as he saw the early Bauhaus. With playful seriousness, and with aesthetic intent, some of the artists at the Bauhaus adapted the non-European exoticism of seemingly archaic/mythical forms in the *African Chair* in order to invent an evolutionary point of origination for

1 Quotation from Fritz Kuhr, 1928, student at the Bauhaus 1923–1927, member of the wall-painting workshop 1928–1929.

2 Hans M. Wingler, *Das Bauhaus: 1919–1933; Weimar, Dessau, Berlin und die Nachfolge in Chicago seit 1937* (Bramsche, 1962; Cologne, 2002).

3 Christoph Wagner (ed.), *Das Bauhaus und die Esoterik: Johannes Itten, Paul Klee, Wassily Kandinsky* (Bielefeld, 2005).

4 Ibid., pp. 16–17, 37.

their own art. In the same year, a response came in the form of Breuer's purely geometric tubular steel furniture, which emerged from a very different Bauhaus milieu. Current research now makes it clear that, on an international level, avant-garde artists of this period, such as Russian Suprematist Kazimir Malevich, explicitly reflected the changes in visual culture in the 1920s. This can be seen, for example, in the photographic documentation in Malevich's book *The Non-Objective World*—written between 1923 and 1926 and published in 1927 as the eleventh in the Bauhaus Books series—which attempts to distinguish the "environment […] which stimulates the Futurist" from the Suprematists' conception of the landscape of the lifeworld:[5] images of the Futurist belief in progress based on technology, industrialisation, and speed are juxtaposed with the higher degree of abstraction in Suprematist aerial photographs. By contrast, the traditional visual images of the "environment […] which stimulates the Academician" remain on the level of a hopelessly outdated rural idyll of the kind represented in nineteenth-century painting.[6] Different programmatic views of reality are set out in different pictorial forms, serving as artistic signatures of various avantgarde movements in the early twentieth century. Sometimes Malevich adapted the dating of his works to suit these developmental concepts.

III.

This new research also makes it clear that the widespread esoteric and thoroughly international tendencies at the Weimar Bauhaus were not simply a footnote, but in fact they were supported through an ideological programme and by a broad consensus of Bauhaus artists representing different focuses and movements. The spectrum encompasses a range of international currents in intellectual history, from guild romanticism to freemasonry, theosophy, anthroposophy, astrology, Mazdaznan, and parascience. The Bauhaus and "the esoteric"—these are two sides of a coin that, for some people, would not seem to belong together. But by zooming out a little, we can see—as a counterpoint to the simplistic image of Johannes Itten as a sectarian maverick and Mazdaznan devotee—just how many other Bauhaus artists, among them Walter Gropius,

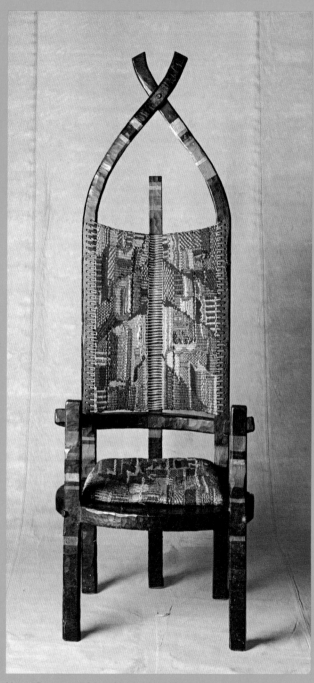

Marcel Breuer and Gunta Stölzl, *African Chair*, 1921

"Avant-Garde Conceptions of Reality", from: Kazimir Malevich,
The Objectless World, Munich, 1927

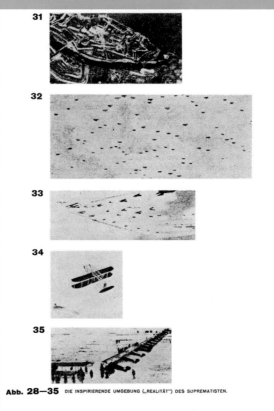

"Avant-Garde Conceptions of Reality",
from: Kazimir Malevich, *The Objectless
World*, Munich, 1927

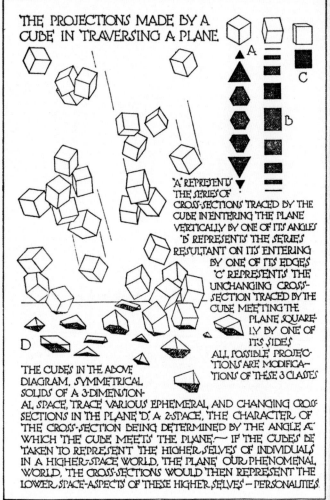

THE PROJECTIONS MADE BY A CUBE IN TRAVERSING A PLANE

'A' REPRESENTS THE SERIES OF CROSS-SECTIONS TRACED BY THE CUBE IN ENTERING THE PLANE VERTICALLY BY ONE OF ITS ANGLES 'B' REPRESENTS THE SERIES RESULTANT ON ITS ENTERING BY ONE OF ITS EDGES 'C' REPRESENTS THE UNCHANGING CROSS-SECTION TRACED BY THE CUBE MEETING THE PLANE SQUARELY BY ONE OF ITS SIDES ALL POSSIBLE PROJECTIONS ARE MODIFICATIONS OF THESE 3 CLASSES

THE CUBES IN THE ABOVE DIAGRAM, SYMMETRICAL SOLIDS OF A 3-DIMENSIONAL SPACE, TRACE VARIOUS EPHEMERAL AND CHANGING CROSS-SECTIONS IN THE PLANE 'D', A 2-SPACE, THE CHARACTER OF THE CROSS-SECTION BEING DETERMINED BY THE ANGLE 'A' WHICH THE CUBE MEETS THE PLANE.— IF THE CUBES BE TAKEN TO REPRESENT THE HIGHER SELVES OF INDIVIDUALS IN A HIGHER-SPACE WORLD, THE PLANE' OUR PHENOMENAL WORLD, THE CROSS-SECTIONS WOULD THEN REPRESENT THE LOWER SPACE-ASPECTS OF THESE HIGHER SELVES — PERSONALITIES.

PLATE 30

MAN THE SQUARE

A HIGHER SPACE PARABLE

"Artful nature has given to the most perfect animal the same six limits as the cube has, most perfectly marked. . . . Man himself is, as it were, a cube."

—*Mysterium Cosmographicum.*
Kepler.

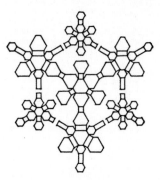

Claude Bragdon, *A Primer of Higher Space (The Fourth Dimension)*, 1913, plate 30

Georg Muche, Gyula Pap, Paul Klee, Karl Peter Röhl, Lothar Schreyer, Gunta Stölzl, and Wassily Kandinsky, were receptive, to varying degrees, to the esoteric and ideological tendencies of the time.[7] At the end of the Weimar years, Gropius certainly felt uneasy about the increasing sectarian activity among the Bauhaus students and teachers. Admittedly, in his Bauhaus manifesto of April 1919, he himself championed the concept of comprehensive human development: at that time Gropius' programme called for the Bauhaus not to "train artists" but to "fashion new human beings".[8]

Itten had already turned to the Mazdaznan doctrine before his appointment to the Bauhaus. But once he had arrived there, his ideological concerns were more pronounced than in any other period of his life, either before or after. At times, even the menu in the cafeteria at the Weimar Bauhaus was geared to the Mazdaznan diet. Numerous Bauhaus teachers and students, such as Sophie van Leer, Georg Muche, Gyula Pap, and Theobald Emil Müller-Hummel, had followed the Mazdaznan teachings to varying degrees. Writing on Wassily Kandinsky, Sixten Ringbom has shown how fundamentally the reading of occult and theosophical writings influenced Kandinsky's concepts of human colour aura, etheric corporeality, and abstraction.[9] Paul Klee's relationship with esotericism is more conflicted: Klee drew on esotericism in many different ways, adopting themes and figures, and indeed it influenced some of the guiding principles of his theory of art; but at the same time he always maintained a distance from ideological doctrines of salvation such as theosophy or anthroposophy, treating them with a certain irony and self-criticism. At the same time, however, he developed a spiritual connection to the world of numbers, a relationship that assumes a blatantly esoteric character in his contact with Neopythagorean worldviews. Bauhaus figures such as Itten and Gropius, along with certain Italian Futurists and Russian Suprematists, were interested in the new esoteric concepts of space and time that were then prevalent on the international scene. American Claude Bragdon,[10] for example, presented them in his seminal theosophical text *A Primer of Higher Space (The Fourth Dimension)*, first published in 1913.

Bragdon, who was born in Ohio in 1866 and died in New York City in 1946, was an American architect, author, and theosophist, whose work was taken up in various ways by the avant-garde. His work proposes nothing less than the dissolution of the classical Euclidean concept of three-dimensional perspectival space, instead viewing it as just one of many projections. Modernism is rife with paradoxes: one striking instance of this is Bragdon's foreword to Louis Sullivan's book *The Autobiography of an Idea* in 1924, which summed up the aesthetic imperative of the Bauhaus in just three words, "form follows function".[11] Walter Gropius, of course, also had Sullivan's seminal text on his shelves. His copy of the book is now in the Bauhaus Archive in Berlin, so it can be assumed that he was also familiar with Bragdon's ideas.

IV.

It is noteworthy that the exercises Itten created for the preliminary course, which are still used around the world at art academies today,[12] are recorded in much more detail in the Viennese diaries written between 1916 and 1919 than in the Weimar diaries. In the Viennese years, Itten outlined almost all the artistic and theoretical aspects that he would later implement at the Bauhaus: rhythm and harmony, the doctrine of polarities, colour theory, forms of expression, analyses of old masters, and time-space movement as a theme. Internationality can be found here on every level: "I must have the students invent forms of expression. For example, by representing the venomous nastiness of the Australian funnel-web spider."[13] Itten was in the habit of linking these exercises in with a study of the old masters, a heuristic attempt to acquaint his students with the entirety of world art, complete with its "formal characteristics": "Contrast between Titian and Giotto, El Greco—Memling, Baroque—Egyptian and Indian, Delacroix—Gothic, Rembrandt—Negros"; "Contrast in the contour of a Negro sculpture and an Egyptian sculpture. The Negro work is intense—rich in contrast, Egyptian, more two-dimensional than the German Old Masters."[14] In his 1917 list of conceptual keywords, Itten clearly did not use the nomenclature we would use today, but his widespread mention of "Negro sculpture" was typical of the time, albeit often

5 Kasimir Malevich, *The Non-Objective World* (Mineola, NY, 1986), p. 23.

6 Ibid. p. 22.

7 Veit Loers (ed.), *Okkultismus und Avantgarde: Von Munch bis Mondrian 1900–1915*, exh. cat. Schirn-Kunsthalle Frankfurt (Ostfildern, 1995).

8 See Walter Gropius's address to the students of the Bauhaus in July 1919 in Wingler, *Das Bauhaus*, pp. 45–6.

9 Sixten Ringbom, *The Sounding Cosmos: A Study in the Spiritualism of Kandinsky and the Genesis of Abstract Painting* (Åbo, 1970); Wagner, *Das Bauhaus und die Esoterik*, pp. 47–54.

10 Claude Bragdon, *A Primer of Higher Space (The Fourth Dimension)* (Rochester, NY, 1913); Linda Dalrymple Henderson, "Claude Bragdon, the Fourth Dimension, and Modern Art in Cultural Context", in Eugenia Ellis and Andrea Reithmayr (eds.), *Claude Bragdon and the Beautiful Necessity*, exh. cat. (Rochester, NY, 2010); Henderson, *The Fourth Dimension and Non-Euclidean Geometry in Modern Art* (Princeton, 1983).

11 Louis H. Sullivan, *The Autobiography of an Idea* (New York, 1924), p. 258.

12 Johannes Itten, *Mein Vorkurs am Bauhaus: Gestaltungs- und Formenlehre* (Ravensburg, 1963).

problematic and widespread—we find it too in Carl Einstein's book *Negro Sculpture*, published in 1915.[15] Admittedly, Itten always treats African art with due appreciation, putting it on a level with works by Cézanne, Rembrandt, the Egyptians, or "Gothic artists" as one of art history's exemplary forms of expression.[16] Teaching in Krefeld in the winter of 1933, Itten was still praising "African dances" as paradigmatic "rhythm", as the "beginning of a living order"—despite the long shadow already cast by the Nazi takeover. "It must invariably be the basis of all designs. For it is the law of life," he wrote.[17] The special rhythm that, in Itten's view, determines African art must be empathically felt in one's own artistic works. "Rhythm counts. Nude drawing. Let your hand resonate: make music"[18]. The aim of the rhythmic exercises was to "translate the movements of the nude into pure hand-arm movements", as a "formal effect", as "emotional stenograms".[19] Itten repeatedly had his pupils draw such stenograms, convinced that these are "pure products of the personality".[20] The fact that in this section of his notes Itten combines his artistic reflections with a written copy of the Hindu Hymn of Creation from the tenth mandala of the *Rigveda*[21]— which he included three years later in the Bauhaus almanac *Utopia*, using Bruno Adler's translation[22]—once again documents how far he had developed his artistic ideas based on an exploration of world art.

V.

Itten's interest in Indian art is recorded in his early diary entries: following on from the major nineteenth-century models of teleological history such as Hegel's *Aesthetics*,[23] he attempted to observe art's development in world history by assigning Indian art its own significance. Itten's lecture "Über Komposition" (On Composition)—delivered on 7 May 1917 to the Austrian Association of Women Artists in Vienna and on 21 May 1917 to the Institute of Art History at the University of Vienna[24]— documents this appreciation of Indian art as a specific part of world art history. Itten understands the "work of art as a living entity, both animated and stimulating, from which man creates an organism in the work using word, sound, and form."[25] At the beginning of this long process of cultural and historical

13 Tagebuch [diary] X, p. 7, in Eva Badura-Triska (ed.), *Johannes Itten: Tagebücher*, vol. 1, p. 377.

14 Ibid., p. 25, 1:381.

15 Carl Einstein, *Negerplastik* (Leipzig, 1915).

16 Tagebuch X, pp. 20–25, 1:380–81.

17 Johannes Itten, Tagebuch Krefeld, sheet 438, Kunstmuseum Bern, Johannes-Itten-Stiftung.

18 Tagebuch X, p. 25, 1:381.

19 Tagebuch X, pp. 26–7, 24 January 1918, 1:382.

20 Tagebuch X, pp. 49–51, 1:388–9.

21 Tagebuch XI, pp. 6, 9, 1:396–7.

22 Bruno Adler (ed.), *Utopia: Dokumente der Wirklichkeit* (Weimar, 1921), pp. 11–12.

23 Georg W. F. Hegel, *Vorlesungen über die Ästhetik*, vols. 1–3 (Suhrkamp, 1986).

Johannes Itten, *Diary IX*, Vienna, Spring 1919, pp. 152–3

development, Itten sees Indian art as high
culture, comparable to Egyptian culture
for example, and superior to contemporary
art in a number of respects:
"The early Indians were extremely sensitive,
keen of eye and keen of ear, their youthful
senses close to the trajectory of the primal
movement. Their instinctive creative power was
immense compared to our own. The Indian
knows only rhythm, infinitely intertwined linear
rhythm, this movement steadily surging
and streaming in chaos. Like this perhaps:
Please focus your attention on the movement
of the hand rather than on the stroke that
results from it. Look to feel the movement."[26]
This idea of "feeling the movement" articulates
the artistic programme with which Itten was
to make his mark at the Bauhaus in his
"Analyses of the Old Masters" in the *Utopia*
almanac. He seems to have made a direct
correlation between the feeling evoked
by Indian art's "infinitely intertwined linear
rhythm" and his own drawing at the time.
One may criticise Itten's ambition in this
lecture, as he attempts to integrate Indian art
into a comprehensive process of cultural and
historical development, either as a teleological
historical construct or as a racist perpetuation
of colonial ideas of development. In doing
so, he certainly sets out to present Indian art
as a direct forebear of contemporary art: the
"Indian cultural epoch was followed by the
Persian" with its sense of light and dark, and
then the Egyptian with its new idea of propor-
tioning form numerically, etc.[27] By way of
Cézanne and the Cubists, Itten finally reaches
the "Futurist view", to which he ascribes
a "longing to return to the strong emotional
experience of the Indian".[28] Itten's notes and
excerpts on this subject in his Tempelherren-
Tagebuch ("House of the Knights Templar"-
diary) show that one of his focuses at the
Bauhaus was on the philosophical, spiritual,
and intellectual background of Indian culture.[29]
This sheds a new light on why it was Johannes
Itten, and not Walter Gropius, who, in May
1922, received a letter from Stella Kramrisch
in Calcutta proposing an exhibition in India.[30]
Kramrisch had already cultivated contacts
with the painters of the Itten School in Vienna.
In this context, the selection of works, and the
textual commentary that Itten published in the
catalogue of the Indian Society of Oriental Art

24   The lecture has come down
to us in three versions, as an
addendum to Tagebuch II, then
revised in Tagebuch VI, and finally
in a fair copy with supplementary
illustrations: Willy Rotzler (ed.),
Johannes Itten: Werke und Schriften
(Zurich, 1978), pp. 212–9; see
also Badura-Triska, *Johannes Itten*,
vol. 1, pp. 224–39, vol. 2, p. 97.

25   Badura-Triska, *Johannes Itten*,
vol. 1, p. 227.

26   Ibid., p. 228–9.

27   Ibid. For more on this, see
Christoph Wagner, "Klees 'Reise
ins Land der besseren Erkenntnis':
Die Ägyptenreise und die Arbeiten
zur 'Cardinal-Progression' im
kulturhistorischen Kontext",
in Uta Gerlach-Laxner and Ellen
Schwinzer (eds.), *Paul Klee: Reisen
in den Süden; "Reisefieber
praecisiert"*, exh. cat. (Ostfildern,
1997), pp. 72–85.

28   Badura-Triska, *Johannes Itten*,
vol. 1, pp. 238–9.

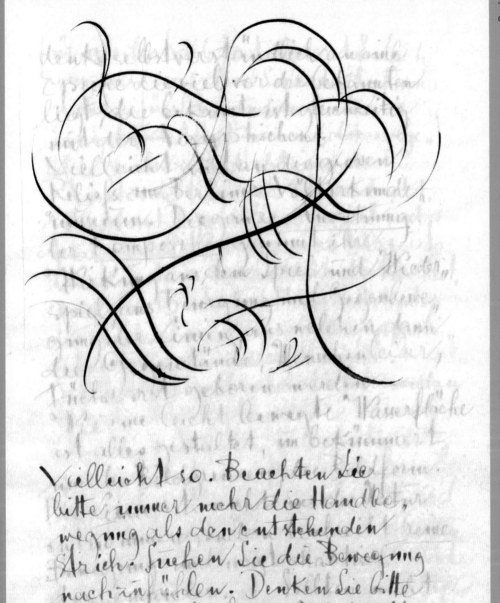

Johannes Itten, Lecture manuscript,
"On Composition" (text copied in another hand with
original sketch by Itten), Vienna, 1917

Vielleicht so. Beachten Sie form
bitte immer mehr die Handbe-
wegung als den entstehenden
Strich. Suchen Sie die Bewegung
nachzufühlen. Denken Sie bitte
dabei an sehr frühe Werte. Ich

18

Johannes Itten, *Hearing and Seeing (Eyes)*, pencil on paper, 1917

to go with the exhibition in India in 1922, is revealing. The conceptual artistic aspiration formulated here, "to express his insight into the rhythm of all visible things, as well as of his own soul",[31] is oddly consistent with the idea that he had formulated back in 1917 of the "longing" for the "rhythm of the Indian perceived as chaotic", the "infinitely intertwined linear rhythm", and the "strong emotional experience of the Indian".[32] It also appears that in this exhibition in Calcutta, Itten set out to match his works with his own paradigm of Indian art—derived from his understanding of cultural history—as a visual language shaped by dynamic rhythm.

VI.

The whole world an ecological Bauhaus? The fact that the etymology of "Bauhaus" can be related to aspects of both ecology and economy—in that the Greek word *oikos* (οἶκος) means not only house but something like household and household community— opens up new thinking with regard to the future international reception of the Bauhaus idea. In retrospect, it has been all too easy for the alternative utopian designs of the Bauhaus to be seen as a response to the degeneration of civilisation, with its surfeit of phenomena, as formulated by Nietzsche at the turn of the century. The "form follows function" paradigm of the Bauhaus has often been reduced to aesthetic norms, but at the same time it specifically puts into practice elements that can be related to the ecological sustainability inherent to an economical use of resources. Many Bauhaus projects—such as the show home Haus Am Horn[33]—can be seen as realisations of just such an *oikos*: the architectural form of the house not only depicts the network of relationships connecting living beings to their environment, such as the economy of laws and the ordering of the household and of economic activity, but also redefines this network in terms of social processes. The Haus Am Horn should certainly be viewed not merely as a normative setting for a "Bauhaus style"; rather, it is the built response to a social and ecological imperative of the early twentieth century. Constructed from innovative materials like prefabricated lightweight building blocks, integrated torfoleum insulation, ceilings made of hollow

29   For example, on pages 165, 168, 177, see Christoph Wagner, *Itten, Gropius, Klee am Bauhaus in Weimar: Utopie und historischer Kontext*, Neue Bauhausbücher, n.s., vol. 3 (Berlin, 2019).

30   Regina Bittner and Kathrin Rhomberg (eds.), *The Bauhaus in Calcutta: An Encounter of the Cosmopolitan Avant-Garde*, exh. cat. (Ostfildern, 2013), p. 69.

31   Ibid., pp. 13–14, as quoted in the copy in Lahore, Pakistan.

32   Badura-Triska, *Johannes Itten*, vol. 1, pp. 229–30.

33   Adolf Meyer, *Ein Versuchshaus des Bauhauses in Weimar*, vol. 3 (Munich, 1925).

ceramic bricks with steel inlays and bituminous sheeting, this *oikos* was intended as a model demonstrating conservation of resources in all areas of construction.

At the same time, this "experimental house"—built according to a design by Georg Muche as part of the first Bauhaus exhibition in the summer of 1923—marks the realignment of the Bauhaus based on the idea of the unity of "art and technology" proclaimed by Walter Gropius and perpetuated right through to the serial buildings in Dessau-Törten and the modular models for Gropius' quick-assembly houses. All these aesthetic interventions at the Bauhaus should also be understood as strategies for sustainability governed by the idea of ecological conservation in the construction process. Even if we cannot readily update the answers that the Bauhaus found to the challenges of its day, it is nevertheless remarkable that they set a global standard in this respect for over fifty years. It is all the more significant since the Bauhaus had to implement its ideas of sustainability not in a climate of economic prosperity or abundance, but in the midst of a global financial crisis and an economy of scarcity.

The idea of the Bauhaus as a kind of "lodge" was intended to bring about the reunification of all the various technical artistic disciplines and create the "unified work of art". Among the numerous Bauhaus teachers and students, it was artists like Paul Klee and Johannes Itten, in particular, who were thoroughly convinced that "only painters can create new architecture". This constellation gave rise to a good many of the Bauhaus' utopian ideals. Their potential is still valid today.

Adolf Meyer, *An Experimental House of the Weimar Bauhaus*, title page, Munich, 1924

THE GLOBAL BAUHAUS

Alexander Klee
Christiane Post
Margret Kentgens-Craig
Silvia Fernández
Enrique Xavier de Anda Alanís
David Maulen and Valérie Hammerbacher
Salma Lahlou
Peter Weibel

Adolf Hölzel—Spiritus Rector
Alexander Klee

Born in Olomouc in 1853, Adolf Hölzel was influenced by the Austro-Hungarian culture of the Habsburg Monarchy. After founding his painting school in Dachau, in Bavaria, in 1887, this was the context in which he systematically developed his own educational system, whose influence can be seen in the teaching for the Bauhaus. His pedagogic system focused on teaching methods and aesthetic questions relating to composition and pictorial structure, culminating in an examination of the representational nature of visual art and of its conceptual focus. The teaching was imparted in the form of lectures followed by practical exercises—in clear contrast to the bookish training at the academies. While students in the preparatory drawing courses were often required to make copies of plaster casts or scenes from nature, Hölzel was primarily interested in analysing artistic methods, and this was the central focus of his work and teaching.[1]

Hölzel believed "that the painter can only represent something using the resources associated with painting, and this is the reason he is a painter. Aside from the technical tools he has at his disposal, he must rely solely on lines, forms, shades, and colours on a finite picture surface to create the image he wants. For him, the tree is not a tree, the man is not a man, the house is not a house; for him, everything consists of lines, of lighter, darker, and coloured forms, of the same planes combined in ever different ways. [...] From our youth we are accustomed to expressing what we see and feel using specific words: this is how we routinely make ourselves understood. In order to express ourselves as painters, we have to re-attune our thinking. [...] Thus art is a language in its own right, unlike our verbal language—the image inhabits a world of its own, which needs to be thoroughly explored. [...] Lines, forms, and colours are merely the alphabet, and teaching the relationships between them provides the grammar. But alphabet and grammar are still not enough to make you a poet. [...] The truly pure art of painting, just like the art of absolute music, proceeds from the means employed, to which its very essence is intimately linked and without which there can be no painting. It can be done without representation, without figures, and include wonderful works that excite the imagination, but without representational means, it is quite unthinkable."[2]

Hölzel describes unrestricted artistic freedom with the term "artistic means"—an expression that had entered common parlance—which the artist is at liberty to use and experiment with. The statement "Art lies in the means employed"[3] reflects his unwavering attitude and can be regarded as one of the fundamental principles of art in the twentieth century. In its radicality and consistency—characteristic features of his work—Hölzel's proposition indicates his shift to embrace an art that can once again make use of the full spectrum of artistic possibilities, since it is not obliged to subordinate itself to any kind of representationalism or illusionism. After his appointment in 1905 to the Royal Academy of Fine Arts in Stuttgart, Hölzel himself was only able to introduce this educational approach to a limited extent, applying it in experimental form during the war. But he aspired to a completely new training system and a new direction in education, which was the polar opposite of the way art was typically taught at the German academies, where there was a heavy emphasis on content. Hölzel observes: "We are now accustomed, from childhood on, to thinking objectively and, so to speak, in literary terms—a mental habit that is also inculcated in schools—in contrast to the manner in which a work of art is created, in whatever way this presents itself to the artistic creator. For whether the final fruit of his work takes the form of a representational rendering or creates artistic harmonies without representationalism—an abstract way of working, you might say—his rendering is *only* ever possible with the means native to painting or his chosen art form. [...] And since for the time being this practical training does not exist anywhere in the requisite thorough manner, a practical *Arbeitsschule* should be created. [...] Such a school, with a focus on manual work, would have multiple purposes to fulfil. It would involve practical instruction in how to work artistically."[4]

Various institutions, such as the Grand Ducal Art School in Weimar under the direction of Henry van de Velde, had set out to combine

1   Alexander Klee, "Adolf Hölzel: Die Stuttgarter Akademie; Ein Epizentrum des künstlerischen Wandels und Schrittmacher der künstlerischen Entwicklung", in Nils Büttner and Angela Ziegler (eds.), *Rücksichten: 250 Jahre Akademie der Bildenden Künste Stuttgart* (Stuttgart, 2011), pp. 103–14.

2   Adolf Hölzel, "Über künstlerische Ausbildung des Malers", *Der Pelikan* 9 (1920), p. 22.

3   Adolf Hölzel, "Einige aphoristische Sätze aus einem demnächst erscheinenden Hefte", in *Hölzel und sein Kreis*, exh. cat. (Stuttgart, 1916), p. 2. Hans Hildebrandt had already pointed out this fundamental shift in Hölzel's work, which first became evident in 1905. See Hans Hildebrandt, *Adolf Hölzel als Zeichner* (Stuttgart, 1913), pp. 11–12.

4   Adolf Hölzel, "Die Schule des Künstlers", *Der Pelikan* 11 (1921), pp. 3–4.

Johannes Itten, Analyses of the old
masters, "The Creation of Eve", French
miniature from the thirteenth century, in
Bruno Adler (ed.), *Utopia. Dokumente der
Wirklichkeit*, Weimar, 1921

5   Michael Siebenbrodt, "Das Staatliche Bauhaus in Weimar – Avantgardeschule für Gestalter 1919–1925", in *Bauhaus Weimar, Entwürfe für die Zukunft* (Stuttgart, 2000), p. 9.

6   Adolf Hölzel, "Gedanken über die Erziehung des künstlerischen Nachwuchses", *Der Pelikan* 10 (1920), pp. 13–14.

7   Alexander Klee, "Forming a Common Language: The Teaching of Drawing in the Habsburg Empire from 1850", in Nino Nanobashvili and Tobias Teutenberg (eds.), *Drawing Education: Worldwide! Continuities—Transfers—Mixtures* (Heidelberg, 2019), pp. 79–96.

8   Alexander Klee, "Formkunst – Phänomen eines Kulturraums", in Agnes Husslein-Arco and Alexander Klee (eds.), *Kubismus – Konstruktivismus – Formkunst*, exh. cat. (Munich, 2016), pp. 23–7.

9   Hölzel, "Die Schule des Künstlers", p. 4.

10   Alexander Klee, "Viribus unitis? Networking im Vielvölkerstaat am Beispiel der Verlegerfamilie Hölzel", in Elisabeth Röhrlich (ed.), *Migration und Innovation um 1900: Perspektiven auf das Wien der Jahrhundertwende* (Vienna, 2016), pp. 442–6, 451.

11   Andreas Haus, "Bauhaus – geschichtlich", in Jeannine Fiedler and Peter Feierabend (eds.), *Bauhaus* (Cologne, 1999), p. 17.

12   Walter Gropius, "Vorschläge zur Gründung einer Lehranstalt als künstlerische Beratungsstelle für Industrie, Gewerbe und Handwerk", in Hans Martin Wingler, *Das Bauhaus* (Cologne, 1975), p. 30; Walter Gropius, "Programm des Staatlichen Bauhauses in Weimar", in ibid., pp. 38–41.

tuition and practice.[5] However, Hölzel's intention was not only to reform the system of instruction but also to rethink the artist's position in general. In his view, anyone can learn the basics of art in just the same way as mathematics or foreign languages can be learned.[6] Such an approach was completely unthinkable in Germany, but it had proved successful in the Austro-Hungarian Empire, where it had been introduced generally in 1873. Here, with the exception of grammar schools with a classical focus on the humanities, freehand drawing lessons were an obligatory part of the curriculum and a requirement for moving up through the educational system. In comparison to Germany, under the Habsburg Monarchy three times as many classroom hours were devoted to drawing lessons, with the special pedagogical training of art teachers lasting three years.[7] There were also major differences in terms of content. Taking mathematics as the starting point—and drawing on the progressive educational proposals championed by people like Johann Heinrich Pestalozzi, Friedrich Fröbel, and, in particular, Johann Friedrich Herbart—teaching was structured along geometrical and mathematical lines based on the firm rejection of the idea of genius.[8] The strong mathematical focus naturally gave drawing an ornamental basis, from which teaching and drawing developed further. Complex interrelationships emerge from the simplest of forms.

Hölzel thus had his sights set on a general reform of artistic instruction, which was to begin well before students entered the academies and schools of arts and crafts. His aim was to forge a connection between artistic research in theory and practice—linked with a training in art—and the school educational system that developed from this.[9] In his inclusion of a system of education for schools, Hölzel's focus diverged from that of the Bauhaus. However, his formalist thinking—which had its origins in the culture of the Habsburgs[10]—coincided with Walter Gropius's intentions,[11] with the result that the concept delineated by Hölzel can be clearly related to the Bauhaus.[12] Here, as postulated by Hölzel, artistic experiments were carried out, thus ensuring the training of a new generation of young masters for the Bauhaus preliminary course, among them Marcel Breuer, Herbert

Bayer, and Josef Albers, who was Johannes Itten's successor.

However, these relationships are not limited to the organisational similarities with the Bauhaus as an educational institution. Without having been a teacher at the Bauhaus, Adolf Hölzel was nonetheless an influential presence in the early phase of the Bauhaus, as embodied in his students Johannes Itten, Oskar Schlemmer, Ida Kerkovius, Vincent Weber, and Ludwig Hirschfeld-Mack. This influence comes through clearly in the idea of the preliminary course and the highly formalised compositional approach, which both Itten and Schlemmer advocated as teachers. Ludwig Hirschfeld-Mack's arrival at the Bauhaus in 1922, as tutor for the theory of colour in the preliminary course, ensured that Hölzel's thinking on the subject more or less held sway at the Bauhaus.[13] Vincent Weber comments, "Of course Kandinsky knew Hölzel fairly well. He held a colour seminar at the Bauhaus, at which Hölzel's colour theories were often the subject of discussion. Itten, Kerkovius, Hirschfeld, Schlemmer, and I were students of Hölzel. So you can imagine the degree to which Hölzel's influence dominated the lessons on colour at the Bauhaus."[14]

Thus, the Bauhaus probably proved to be the most effective disseminator of Hölzel's thinking. Johannes Itten played a crucial role in shaping the Bauhaus preliminary course from 1919 to 1922. The tasks he defined for it included encouraging individuality and creative artistic talent, with students developing a feeling for the materials and knowing and exploring the basic laws of pictorial design, form, and colour.[15]

Itten adopted Hölzel's approach of having students confront the fundamentals of artistic thought by delivering lectures accompanied by a slideshow, in which he elucidated works by Titian, Botticelli, Dürer, and Rubens, with a focus on the basic principles informing their composition.[16] In 1901, he presented his view of composition in *Ver Sacrum*, the magazine of the Vienna Secession, under the expressive title "Über Formen und Massenvertheilung im Bilde" (On Forms and the Distribution of Mass in Images),[17] a means of analysing images that Itten continued in his "Analysen Alter Meister" (Analyses of the Old Masters)[18] and in his diary "Beiträge zu einem Kontrapunkt der

James Liberty Tadd, *Neue Wege zur künstlerischen Erziehung* (New Methods in Education), Leipzig, 1903

13   Peter Stasny, "Biographie", in *Ludwig Hirschfeld-Mack: Bauhäusler und Visionär*, exh. cat. (Ostfildern-Ruit, 2000), p. 169.

14   Quoted in Wolfgang Venzmer, *Adolf Hölzel: Leben und Werk; Monographie mit Verzeichnis der Ölbilder, Glasfenster und ausgewählter Pastelle* (Stuttgart, 1982), p. 206, n. 185.

15   Willy Rotzler, *Johannes Itten: Werke und Schriften* (Zurich, 1978), p. 226.

16   Transcripts of the lectures including analyses of specific images by artists such as Giotto, Titian, and Leonardo have come down to us in largely complete and consistent form, based on notes taken by Bruno May (c.1905), Luise Deicher (1910), Lily Hildebrandt (1910–1911), Clara Fauser (1912), and Albert Mueller (1914).

17   Adolf Hölzel, "Über Formen und Massenvertheilung im Bilde", *Ver Sacrum* 4 (1901), pp. 243–54.

18   Johannes Itten, "Analysen Alter Meister", in Bruno Adler (ed.), *Utopia: Dokumente der Wirklichkeit* (Weimar, 1921), pp. 29ff.

Adolf Hölzel, Rhythmic circular forms, graphite on paper, c.1930

Drawing class in Itten's school, left- and right-handed drawing— designed to develop a sense of symmetry, 1929

Paula Stockmar, Portrait of Johannes Itten
in painter's smock with golden compass and
colour-star, 1921

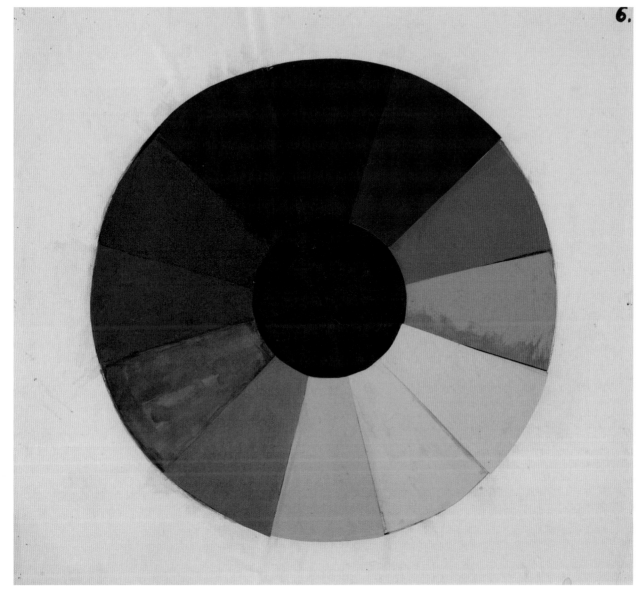

Adolf Hölzel, Twelve-part chromatic color circle, collage, ink, pencil, gouache, and colored paper on board, n.d.

Oskar Schlemmer, Analysis of the painting of the
Vorübergehender (Passing Figure), drawing, 1929

19   Johannes Itten, *Tagebuch. Beiträge zu einem Kontrapunkt der bildenden Kunst* (Berlin, 1930), p. 33.

20   See Rainer K. Wick, *Bauhaus Kunstschule der Moderne* (Stuttgart, 2000), p. 96; Katharina Hadding, "Johannes Itten and Ida Kerkovius: Eine Künstlerfreundschaft im Zeichen der Lehre Adolf Hölzels", in Christa Lichtenstern and Christoph Wagner (eds.), *Johannes Itten und die Moderne* (Stuttgart, 2003), pp. 74–5.

21   A list of books owned by Hölzel can be found in his estate at the Adolf-Hölzel-Stiftung in Stuttgart. It includes James Liberty Tadd's *Neue Wege zur künstlerischen Erziehung der Jugend* (Leipzig, 1903).

22   Vincent Weber on Adolf Hölzel, in Harald Siebenbrodt (ed.), *Vincent Weber: Zauberteppich*, exh. cat. (Weimar, 2002), p. 38.

23   Hölzel specified that hand exercises should be part of any future training in "Die Schule des Künstlers", pp. 7–8.

24   Hölzel, "Gedanken über die Erziehung des künstlerischen Nachwuchses", p. 14.

25   Ekkehard Mai, "Kunstakademien im Wandel: Zur Reform der Künstlerausbildung im 19. Jahrhundert; Die Beispiele Berlin und München", in Hans M. Wingler, *Kunstschulreform* (Berlin, 1977), p. 51.

bildenden Kunst" (Contributions to a Counterpoint of Visual Art).[19] This involved researching the deployment of chiaroscuro and geometric composition in the history of art. It was the art which had come before—which both Hölzel and Itten analysed on the basis of model examples—rather than conceptual brilliance and inspiration that acted as the substrate. However, the study of feeling conducted by Itten contrasted with Hölzel's structural analysis inasmuch as it was more strongly influenced by emotion.[20]

As with Hölzel, the lectures in Itten's preliminary course were followed by practice sessions, the fruit of which is strongly reminiscent of the works that came out of Hölzel's class. Thus the collages that Hölzel set store by in his exploration of forms and composition were also used in the preliminary course, but with a stronger focus on their materiality. Hölzel's interest in ornament was also based on a fundamental pedagogical concern: the training of a sense of form. Here, Hölzel also included James Liberty Tadd's empirical findings, which were described in his book *New Methods in Education*.[21] The book presents intuitive form-finding as part of the curriculum. Students created symmetrical ornamental figures while painting with both hands. This kind of practice coincided with Hölzel's morning exercises, the daily 1,000 lines[22] which he was legendary for, and his free compositions, although the intention here was not to design decorative elements, as was the case with Tadd.[23] Hölzel thus stipulated that his training should involve strengthening the hand as an organ of feeling: "In painting, our organ of perception is the eye—art involves looking. The hand is our organ of feeling. By training our eye and simultaneously fulfilling its demands, we will be acting in accordance with our perception. The hand will have to support the perception in its expression. Manual exercises of various kinds were thus also included in the experimental plan for an elementary school: exercises to train and strengthen the arm and hand were practised at length on large boards."[24] Itten adopted this into his teaching by having his pupils carry out similar graphic and gymnastic exercises.[25]

Just as Itten extended Hölzel's theory of colour and form by adding subjective modes of perception, Oskar Schlemmer was also influenced by the stimulus he had received from Hölzel. Schlemmer, who was appointed to the Bauhaus in 1920, introduced the importance of proportion into his courses devoted to the topic of "Man". The ideas that Hölzel had imparted in his lessons on constructive composition and the golden mean are in evidence here as well. Hölzel also called for training in composition, which figured in art history as well. This was to be part of any future schooling: "If we find that the old masters used lines and dots in circular form in their pictures, we can be sure that they really used the compass and did not merely obtain these results by virtue of their highly developed perception. We cannot rely on sensation with any degree of certainty. It takes an extraordinary amount of practice to be able to correctly draw a circle or a square freehand."[26]

When Itten resigned in 1923, his former pupil Josef Albers took over the preliminary course. Under him, the focus and intent of the preliminary course shifted once again, with the emphasis now on research into the technical and aesthetic possibilities of the material. Hölzel's realisation that the artistic means is a language free of any literary content, one that can dispense with depiction, was systematically developed by Albers. Hölzel's artistic concept of the "autochthonous power of artistic means"[27] opened up the possibilities for experimental freedom. It was precisely this interplay of teaching, practice, experiment, and practical implementation—which Hölzel had tried out in his class in Stuttgart—that was put into effect at the Bauhaus.

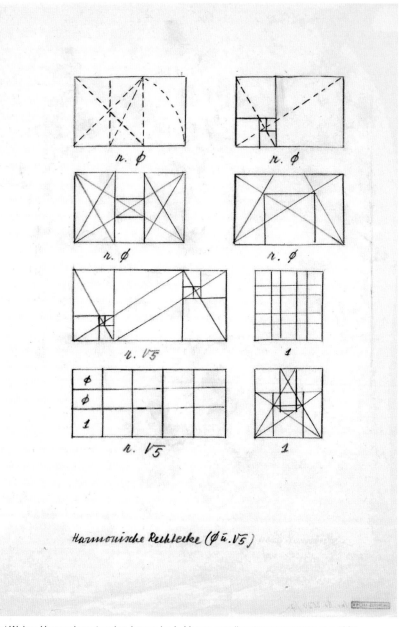

Vincent Weber, Harmonic rectangles, lesson by A. Meyer, pencil on transparent paper, c.1921

26 Adolf Hölzel, "Einige aphoristische Sätze aus einem demnächst erscheinenden Hefte", p. 8; see also Hölzel, "Über künstlerische Ausbildung des Malers", *Der Pelikan* 9 (1920), p. 24.

27 Adolf Hölzel, "Über künstlerische Ausdrucksmittel und deren Verhältnis zu Natur und Bild", *Kunst für Alle* 20 (1904), p. 129.

The Moscow Higher State Art and Technical Workshops (VKhUTEMAS) and the Bauhaus

Christiane Post

Two of the most innovative avant-garde art schools of the 1920s were created at almost the same time: the Bauhaus (1919–1933) and the VKhUTEMAS (1920–1930). Both were informed by new approaches to artistic training and a radical educational system.

The Moscow Higher State Art and Technical Workshops, VKhUTEMAS,[1] were established on 29 November 1920.[2] They emerged from the First and Second Free State Art Studios (SGKhM), established one year after the October Revolution as part of a programme of reform that changed the way art was taught and led to the reorganisation of Russia's art schools. The SGKhM developed from the Imperial Central Stroganov School of Arts and Crafts (SCKhPU) and the Moscow School of Painting, Sculpture, and Architecture (MUZhVZ).[3] In its founding document—the Decree of the Council of People's Commissars Concerning the Moscow Higher State Art and Technical Workshops signed by Vladimir Ulyanov (Lenin)—VKhUTEMAS was described as a special school combining art, technology, and industry. From the very beginning, the aim was to train "artists with higher qualifications for industry".[4] Meanwhile, Walter Gropius's "Programme of the State Bauhaus in Weimar", published in 1919, set out to "reunify all the disciplines of practical art—sculpture, painting, handicrafts, and the crafts—as inseparable components of a new architecture.[5] In the founding manifesto of the Bauhaus, he explicitly called for a return to craftsmanship.

Based on the subjects offered by its predecessors as well as the school's new objectives, VKhUTEMAS was organised into eight faculties: painting, sculpture, architecture, graphics, textiles, ceramics, metalwork, and woodwork.[6] Similar to the Bauhaus preliminary course, the preparatory department covering the fundamentals offered a one-year basic course to students of all faculties as an introduction to the essential principles of art and supplementary academic disciplines.[7]

While an average of 150 students per semester were enrolled at the Bauhaus,[8] VKhUTEMAS registered 2,000 students to start with, and subsequently about 1,500.[9] The reason for the high number of students was the free and equal access to the new schools that was made possible by the October Revolution of 1917. Although women in nineteenth-century Russia were "encouraged" to train in the arts and were later able to study at the art academies "regardless of class or social standing",[10] in many cases it proved impossible for them to enter the field of architecture in pre-revolutionary Russia.[11] In the first years after the revolution, the number of female students increased, as a large number were now able to study at the reformed art schools and colleges.[12] Likewise, as Bauhaus researcher Magdalena Droste wrote, "the new Weimar Constitution guaranteed women unrestricted freedom of study. Academies could no longer [...] refuse women entry." But in the early days of the Bauhaus, access to courses was made more difficult for women as a matter of principle, and "those who overcame the first hurdles were forcibly channelled into the weaving workshop":[13] In total, around forty women studied architecture at the Bauhaus,[14] and between 1927 and 1933 there were only sixteen in the building department.[15] VKhUTEMAS had over ten times as many students as the Bauhaus, with a teaching staff of more than 200 professors, including lecturers.[16] In addition to the "academics", the faculty also comprised avant-garde artists such as Wassily Kandinsky, El Lissitzky, Lyubov Popova, Aleksandr Rodchenko, Varvara Stepanova, and Vladimir Tatlin, as well as the architects Nikolai Ladovsky, Moisei Ginzburg, and Aleksandr Vesnin—exponents of "rationalism" and constructivism. The rectors were the sculptor Efim Ravdel (1920–1923), the graphic artist Vladimir Favorsky (1923–1926), and art theorist Pavel Novitsky (1926–1930), who was a key influence on the direction taken by the art school.[17]

The standard programme of study at VKhUTEMAS initially lasted four years, of which one year was devoted to the basic course and three years to studies in the specialist departments.[18] This subsequently increased to five years, with the basic course extended by one year. The last six months were reserved for the diploma thesis.[19] A variety of art subjects—also referred to as "disciplines" and by Lyubov Popova as "a new objective method

1 On the reception history of VKhUTEMAS (Vysshie Gosudarstvennye Khudozhestvenno-Tekhnichskie Masterskie), see Christian Schädlich, "Die Moskauer Höheren künstlerisch-technischen Werkstätten und das Bauhaus", *Wissenschaftliche Zeitschrift der Hochschule für Architektur und Bauwesen Weimar* 5/6 (1976), pp. 472–5; Selim O. Khan-Magomedov, *VKhUTEMAS – VKhUTEIN* (Moscow, 1990); *VHUTEMAS: Moscou 1920–1930*, 2 vols. (Paris, 1990); Christina Lodder, "The VKhUTEMAS and the Bauhaus", in Gail Harrison Roman and Virginia Hagelstein Marquardt (eds.), *The Avant-Garde Frontier: Russia Meets the West, 1910–1930* (Gainesville, FL, 1992), pp. 196–240; Selim O. Khan-Magomedov, *VKhUTEMAS*, 2 vols. (Moscow, 1995 and 2000); Larisa Ivanovna Ivanova-Veén (ed.), *VKhUTEMAS – VKhUTEIN: Moskva – Leningrad; 1920–1930, Uchebnye raboty iz sobraniia Muzeia MARKhI*, (Moscow, 2010); Irina V. Chepkunova (ed.), *VKhUTEMAS: Mysl' material'na; Katalog kollektsii studencheskikh rabot VKhUTEMAS iz sobraniia Gosudarstvennogo muzeia arkhitektury im. A. V. Shchuseva* (Moscow, 2011); Berliner Festspiele and Martin-Gropius-Bau (eds.), *WChUTEMAS: Ein russisches Labor der Moderne; Architekturentwürfe 1920–1930* (Berlin, 2015).

Exhibition of student works in the discipline of "Space" in the basic course of
VKhUTEMAS/VKhUTEIN in Moscow, 1927/1928

Aleksandr Vesnin, Design of the external façade of VKhUTEMAS
on the occasion of the tenth anniversary of the October Revolution,
Moscow, no date (1927)

2   See "Dekret Soveta Narodnykh Komissarov: O Moskovskikh Vysshikh Gosudarstvenno-Technichskich Masterskikh" (1920), in Rabochee i Krest'ianskoe Pravitel'stvo, Sobranie uzakonenii i rasporiazhenii Rabochego i Krest'ianskogo Pravitel'stva, Moscow, 19 December 1920, no. 98, pp. 540–1, Art. 522.

3   See Khan-Magomedov, VKhUTEMAS, vol. 2, pp. 331–43. Like the Bauhaus, VKhUTEMAS also came out of the merger of an art college with a school of arts and crafts. The college buildings were located at Rozhdestvenka 11 and Miasnitskaia 21.

4   See Dekret 1920, p. 540.

5   Hans M. Wingler, Bauhaus: Weimar, Dessau, Berlin, Chicago, ed. Joseph Stein, trans. Wolfgang Jabs and Basil Gilbert, rev. ed. (Cambridge, MA, 1976), p. 32.

6   See "Polozhenie o Gosudarstvennykh Moskovskikh Vysshikh Chudozhestvennykh Masterskikh" (1920), in Khan-Magomedov, VKhUTEMAS, p. 342; VHUTEMAS, vol. 1, p. 220. It should be noted that the number of faculties and the names assigned to them changed in some cases between 1920 and 1930 and that some of the faculties had sub-departments.

7   The VKhUTEMAS department running the basic course (Podgotovitel'no-ispytatel'noe otdelenie) was initially intended to offer lectures in fields such as "drawing, painting, modelling, technical drawings, descriptive geometry, planning drawings, anatomy, art history, physics, chemistry, and mathematics." See Khan-Magomedov, VKhUTEMAS, p. 342. The length of the basic course at VKhUTEMAS varied, just as it did at the Bauhaus.

8   See Patrick Rössler and Anke Blümm, "Soft Skills and Hard Facts: A Systematic Assessment of the Inclusion of Women at the Bauhaus", in Elizabeth Otto and Patrick Rössler (eds.), Bauhaus Bodies. Gender, Sexuality, and Body Culture in Modernism's Legendary Art School (New York, 2019), p. 9.

9   See Schädlich, "Die Moskauer Höheren künstlerisch-technischen Werkstätten und das Bauhaus", p. 473.

10   See Ada Raev, Russische Künstlerinnen der Moderne (1870–1930): Historische Studien, Kunstkonzepte, Weiblichkeitsentwürfe (Munich, 2002), pp. 86–113, esp.: 91, 97.

11   See Selim O. Khan-Magomedov, Pervye vypuski molodykh storonnikov arkhitekturnogo avangarda: MPI – MIGI (1920–1924) (Moscow, 1997).

12   See ibid.; Larisa Ivanovna Ivanova-Veèn (ed.), VKhUTEMAS – VKhUTEIN: Moskva – Leningrad; 1920–1930, Vypuskniki (Moscow, 2010).

13   Magdalena Droste, bauhaus 1919–1933 (Cologne, 2019), pp. 84–7, 158–62; see Rössler and Blümm, "Soft Skills and Hard Facts", pp. 7–12. Restrictions on admission to study programmes and most of the workshops as well as the establishment of a class for women thwarted "absolute gender equality".

14   See Rössler and Blümm, "Soft Skills and Hard Facts", p. 10.

15   Corinna Isabel Bauer, "Bauhaus- und Tessenow-Schülerinnen: Genderaspekte im Spannungsverhältnis von Tradition und Moderne", PhD diss., University of Kassel, 2003, p. 58.

16   See Khan-Magomedov, VHUTEMAS, vol. 1, pp. 224–6.

17   See ibid., pp. 93–95.

18   See Dekret 1920, p. 540.

19   Khan-Magomedov, VHUTEMAS, vol. 1, p. 214. In the academic year 1926/27 the basic course was shortened to one year, and in 1929 it was further reduced to six months.

20   Lyubov Popova, "Zur Frage der neuen Ausbildungsmethoden an unseren Kunstschulen", (1921), in Magdalena Dabrowski (ed.), Ljubow Popowa 1889–1924 (Munich, 1991), p. 158.

21   See Christina Lodder, Russian Constructivism (New Haven, CT; London, 1983), p. 22–129.

22   See Lyubov Popova and Aleksandr Vesnin, "Discipline No. 1 – 'Colour'", in Dmitri V. Sarabianov and Natalia L. Adaskina, Popova (New York, 1990), p. 368, as well as Popova's remarks on the course content and teaching methods, pp. 369–77; see Khan-Magomedov, VHUTEMAS, vol. 1, pp. 261–6.

23   See Aleksandr Rodchenko, "Discipline: Graphic Construction on a Plane" (1921), in Alexander N. Lavrentiev (ed.), Aleksandr Rodchenko: Experiments for the Future; Diaries, Essays, Letters, and Other Writings (New York, 2005), pp. 187–9; Galina D. Tschitschagowa, "Die Jahre der WChUTEMAS", in Varvara Rodchenko (ed.), A. M. Rodtschenko: Aufsätze, autobiographische Notizen, Briefe, Erinnerungen, (Dresden, 1993), pp. 196–204; Khan-Magomedov, VHUTEMAS, vol. 1, pp. 267–78.

of analysing the formal elements of 'art'"[20]— were covered in the basic course.[21] These included, among other things, colour and form theory as well as construction. The discipline of "colour" was taught by Lyubov Popova and Aleksandr Vesnin, who regarded colour as an "independent organisational principle of painting" and took a critical approach to the theory of colour, focusing on the chromatic spectrum and the tonality and materiality of colour.[22] "Construction", or rather "Graphic Construction on the Plane", was taught by Aleksandr Rodchenko on the basis of geometric still lifes and structural assignments.[23] Avant-garde artists also covered for the other disciplines.[24]

In the academic year 1922/23, the basic training was centred on four disciplines—"colour", "space", "volume", and "graphics"—and in the autumn of 1923 the "preparatory course focusing on formal analysis" was introduced as a cross-faculty, interdisciplinary foundation programme for students from all subjects.[25] Developed by Nikolai Ladovsky on the basis of psychophysics as a teaching programme at his United Left Workshops (Obmas)[26]—part of the VKhUTEMAS faculty of architecture— the "Psychoanalytic Method" was adopted as the discipline "Space" in the department running the basic course and served as a preliminary introduction for students of all faculties.[27] His teaching method was based on design tasks that were divided into two parts and included an "abstract" as well as a "productive" assignment—along with its execution in the form of models.[28]

In 1923, Nikolai Ladovsky founded the Association of New Architects (ASNOVA),[29] which emerged from the Architects' Working Group at the Institute of Artistic Culture (INKhUK).[30] INKhUK was a research institute focused on art and science with a cooperative committee, to which Wassily Kandinsky and Aleksandr Rodchenko belonged. The artistic research at INKhUK and VKhUTEMAS was closely interwoven. INKhUK members were also on the teaching staff at VKhUTEMAS. Against the background of the discussions on constructivism and production art conducted at the Institute of Artistic Culture[31]—the Constructivists' Working Group had been founded at INKhUK in 1921—the "question of the organisation of a production workshop"[32]

Lyubov Popova and Aleksandr Vesnin with students at VKhUTEMAS in Moscow, 1922

Ljubov Popova, Textile design, gouache and ink on paper, 1923/1924

was raised in the VKhUTEMAS department running the basic course and this approach was then introduced into the curriculum in those departments focused on productivist art. Aleksandr Rodchenko, who had been appointed to the metalwork faculty (Metfak), taught technical drawing and developed teaching programmes for creating products in the metalworking industry.[33] Varvara Stepanova, who had worked together with Lyubov Popova to design fabric samples for the textile industry in the First State Cotton-Printing Factory, also taught in the VKhUTEMAS textile faculty in 1924/25.[34] Apart from her, other staff included El Lissitzky and Vladimir Tatlin: beginning in the 1926/27 academic year, El Lissitzky taught in the woodwork faculty (Derfak), while Tatlin was an instructor in metalwork and woodwork (Dermetfak).[35]

In the mid-1920s, a new approach was established in the architecture faculty alongside "rationalism"—this was constructivism, or the so-called functional method, represented by Aleksandr Vesnin and Moisei Ginzburg.[36] In late 1925, the two founded the Association of Contemporary Architects (OSA), followed in 1926 by the journal *Contemporary Architecture* (SA),[37] which regularly reported on the Bauhaus.[38]

At the same time, Nikolai Ladovsky set up the Psychotechnical Laboratory, as it was called, in the architecture faculty, where experiments were carried out on the psychology of perception.[39] The student research projects and diploma theses that came out of his workshop and that of Aleksandr Vesnin were published internationally,[40] including Ivan Leonidov's 1927 design for the "V. I. Lenin Institute for Library Sciences in the Sparrow Hills in Moscow" (Aleksandr Vesnin's architecture workshop) and Lyubov Zalesskaya's 1929 design for the "Park of Culture and Leisure in Moscow" (Nikolai Ladovsky's architecture workshop). The Museum of Painterly Culture (MZhK) was also part of VKhUTEMAS and the system of art education.[41] It had been founded in 1919 by avant-garde artists as part of a network of modern art museums, most of which were affiliated with art schools—the museum's first directors were Wassily Kandinsky and Aleksandr Rodchenko.[42]

In 1927, VKhUTEMAS was renamed the Higher State Art and Technical Institute

24   See Lodder, *Russian Constructivism*, pp. 122–9; Khan-Magomedov, *VHUTEMAS*, vol. 1, pp. 255–84. It should be noted that the number of disciplines offered in the department running the basic course and the titles given to them changed between 1920 and 1923. The teaching staff also changed: Aleksandr Drevin, Aleksandra Ekster, Ivan Kliun, Aleksandr Osmerkin, and Nadezhda Udaltsova, among others, taught in the "basics" department of the faculty of painting.

25   See Khan-Magomedov, *VHUTEMAS*, vol. 1, pp. 257, 260.

26   See Selim O. Khan-Magomedov, *Psikhoanaliticheskii metod N. Ladovskogovo VKhUTEMASe – VKhUTEINe (Ob-edinennye levye masterskie, psikhotekhnicheskaia laboratoriia)* (Moscow, 1993).

27   See Selim O. Khan-Magomedov, *Ratsionalizm (ratsio-arkhitektura) "formalizm"*, (Moscow, 2007), pp. 143–97; *Nikolai Ladovsky* (Moscow, 2011), pp. 119–224.

28   See Khan-Magomedov, *Nikolai Ladovsky*. The "abstract" assignments addressed topics such as the "geometric properties of form", "mass and weight", "construction", and "space". The "productive/productivist" assignments included the design of a warehouse, a tower for processing lye, a jetty, and a restaurant on the cliff by the sea, as well as a communal house for workers. See Selim O. Chan-Magomedov, *Pioniere der sowjetischen Architektur: Der Weg zur neuen sowjetischen Architektur in den zwanziger und zu Beginn der dreißiger Jahre* (Dresden, 1983), pp. 107–8.

29   See Selim O. Khan-Magomedov, *ASNOVA, OSA i gruppy INKhUKa* (Moscow, 1994); *Ratsionalizm*, pp. 102–37, 198–241.

30   See Selim O. Khan-Magomedov, *INKhUK i rannii konstruktivizm* (Moscow, 1994).

31   On constructivism, see Lodder, *Russian Constructivism*; Selim O. Khan-Magomedov, *Konstruktivizm – koncepciia formoobrazovaniia* (Moscow, 2003). On production art, see Nikolai Tarabukin, *Ot mol'berta k mashine* (Moscow, 1923).

32   See Aleksandr Vesnin, Anton Lavinsky, Lyubov Popova, and Aleksandr Rodchenko, "Zur Frage der Organisation einer Produktionswerkstatt an den VChUTEMAS: Februar 1923", in Hubertus Gaßner and Eckhard Gillen, *Zwischen Revolutionskunst und Sozialistischem Realismus: Dokumente und Kommentare; Kunstdebatten in der Sowjetunion von 1917 bis 1934* (Cologne, 1979), pp. 140–2.

33   See Khan-Magomedov, *VHUTEMAS*, vol. 2, pp. 641–70; Rodchenko, *A. M. Rodtschenko*, pp. 201–12; Khan-Magomedov, *Konstruktivizm*, pp. 240–51, 262–5; Lavrentiev, *Aleksandr Rodchenko*, pp. 189–97; Anke Hennig (ed.), *Über die Dinge. Texte der russischen Avantgarde* (Hamburg, 2010), pp. 115–24.

34   See Alexander Lavrentiev, *Warwara Stepanowa: Ein Leben für den Konstruktivismus*, (Weingarten, 1988), pp. 79–84, 182–4; Sarabianov and Adaskina, *Popova*, pp. 299–304; Christina Lodder, "Lyubov Popova: A Revolutionary Woman Artist", in *Constructive Strands in Russian Art 1914–1937* (London, 2005), pp. 426–57.

35   See Sophie Lissitzky-Küppers, *El Lissitzky: Maler, Architekt, Typograf, Fotograf* (Dresden, 1992), pp. 69–70; Larissa A. Zhadova, *Tatlin* (Weingarten, 1987), pp. 322–3, 327–8; Khan-Magomedov, *Konstruktivizm*, pp. 255–7, 260–1, 266–9; *VKhUTEMAS – VKhUTEIN*, vol. 2, pp. 671–96.

36   See Chan-Magomedov, *Pioniere der sowjetischen Architektur*, pp. 146–96; *Alexander Wesnin und der Konstruktivismus* (Stuttgart, 1987), pp. 144–8; *Konstruktivizm*, pp. 490–2, 518–22; Christiane Post, *Arbeiterklubs als neue Bauaufgabe der sowjetischen Avantgarde* (Berlin, 2004), pp. 29–34, 74–87.

37   The architectural journal *Sovremennaia Arkhitektura* (1926–1930) published by Aleksandr Vesnin and Moisei Ginzburg, in conjunction with an editorial board, had a pragmatic concept and an international focus, making it an exception among the Russian periodicals of the 1920s: its second issue had a bilingual title, which expanded to three languages in the third issue (*Sovremennaia Arkhitektura – Architektur der Gegenwart – L'architecture contem-poraine*). See Khan-Magomedov, *Konstruktivizm*, pp. 480–6; Guido Canella and Maurizio Meriggi (eds.), *SA: Sovremennaja Arkhitektura 1926–1930* (Bari, 2007); Jean-Louis Cohen, *La pjatiletka extraordinaire de Sovremennaja Arkhitektura – Neobychnaia piatiletka Sovremennoi Arkhitektury – Ein ungewöhnlicher Fünfjahrplan der Sovremennaja architektura* (Ekaterinburg, 2010).

38   See *Sovremennaia Arkhitektura* 1 (1926); 6 (1927); 2, 5 (1928).

39   See Nikolai Ladovsky, "Psikho-tekhnicheskaia laboratoriia architektury (v poradke postanovki voprosa)", *Izvestiia ASNOVA* 1 (1926), p. 7; *Arkhitektura i VKhUTEIN* 1 (1929), pp. 2–4; Khan-Magomedov, *Ratsionalizm*, pp. 364–72.

El Lissitzky, Design of the book *Arkhitektura. Raboty arkhitekturnogo fakul'teta VKhUTEMASa. 1920–1927* (Architecture: The Works of the Faculty of Architecture at VKhUTEMAS, 1920–1927), Moscow, 1927

Aleksandr Vesnin, Moisei Ginzburg (editors), *SA. Sovremennaia Arkhitektura. Architektur der Gegenwart. L'architecture contemporaine*, 6, 1927

КОНСТРУКТИВИЗМ КАК МЕТОД ЛАБОРАТОРНОЙ И ПЕДАГОГИЧЕСКОЙ РАБОТЫ•

Понятие, скрываемое за словом „архитектура",— функция эпохи. Каждый исторический период со своим хозяйственным и культурным своеобразием ставит свои специфические задачи, порождает свою целевую установку, вкладывает свое содержание в слово „архитектура".

В конструктивные периоды истории, т. е. в периоды интенсивного формирования новой культуры от архитектора требуются прежде всего изобретение и кристаллизация социальных конденсаторов эпохи, создание новых архитектурных организмов, эту эпоху обслуживающих.

В периоды общественного и культурного застоя и депрессии не может быть речи о создании новых организмов, и архитектору остается возможность декоративного украшения уже давно канонизированных типов.

В первом случае под словом „архитектура" преимущественно понимается искусство организации, изобретения, жизнестроения.

Во втором — искусство декорации и украшения.

Конструктивизм, или функциональный метод, рожден нашей эпохой — эпохой дважды конструктивной: **на базе социальной революции,** выдвинувшей нового потребителя и кристаллизующей новые хозяйственные и общественные взаимоотношения, и **на базе небывалого роста техники,** непрерывных технических завоеваний, создающих исключительные возможности строительства новой жизни.

Наша эпоха конструктивна не только сегодня, как исторический этап, как временный период интенсивнейшего жизнестроительства. Она конструктивна еще и по изменившемуся жизненному темпу, не дающему возможности долго задерживаться на каком-либо этапе и почти изо дня в день несущему новое в своих социальных задачах и хозяйственно-технических возможностях. Вот почему сегодняшнее объяснение понятия „архитектура" возможно только в функциональной архитектуре, в конструктивизме, ставящем архитектору прежде всего **задачу жизнестроения, организации форм новой жизни.**

• Настоящая статья есть схематический план курса **теории архитектуры,** читаемого автором на архитектурном отделении Вхутемаса и МВТУ.

МАСТЕРСКИЕ БАУХАУЗА В ДЕССАУ
АРХИТЕКТОР ВАЛЬТЕР ГРОПИУС

Однако эта задача жизнестроения, задача создания социальных конденсаторов нашей эпохи получает свое завершение лишь кристаллизованная конкретными материальными формами, одетая в плоть и кровь и представляющая собой ряд архитектурных признаков, воздействующих на психику человека и **чувственно им воспринимаемых.** Другими словами, задача жизнестроения, начинаясь организацией форм новой жизни, новых бытовых и трудовых процессов, заканчивается материализацией и оформлением архитектурных объектов—пространственных вместилищ этих форм новой жизни.

В дореволюционной, так называемой „художественной" архитектуре, как и в архитектуре, базирующейся на формальных принципах, неизбежно возникает дуализм противопоставления утилитарной сущности объекта и его оформления.

Конструктивизм как метод стремится к окончательному уничтожению этого дуализма, к абсолютному **монизму,** тем, что:

1) не допускает наличия никаких нерабочих „прибавочных" элементов в оформлении своих социальных конденсаторов;

2) разрешает основные вопросы эмоционального воздействия самим способом организации утилитарно-конструктивного становления;

3) оформляет каждую деталь функционально, т. е. организуя материал вещи исключительно в пределах ее полезного действия.

Таким образом, **целостность монистического устремления конструктивизма сказывается не в отрицании эмоционального воздействия материальных объектов** (как это обычно принято инкриминировать конструктивизму), **а в организации этого воздействия в самом процессе утилитарно-конструктивного становления их.**

Однако методологически, в целях лабораторной проработки всего производственного процесса архитектора, конструктивизм прибегает подобно многим другим научным дисциплинам **к способу лабораторного рассечения одной реакции,** т. е. **ко временной изоляции одной части по существу целостного процесса от других** для получения наиболее благоприятных условий анализа. Этот принцип лабораторного рассечения реакции существенно отличается от абстрактного изучения вопросов тем, что последнее состоит в отвлеченной работе над отвлеченными элементами, в то время как лабораторное рассечение есть искусственная изоляция реального элемента из конкретного целого, после окончания лабораторной работы восстанавливаемого во временно нарушенной целостности. Следуя принципу лабораторного рассечения реакции, конструктивизм в процессе своей теоретической работы расчленяет единый процесс работы архитектора на ряд отдельных, искусственно изолируемых частей.

I

Первым своим объектом конструктивизм, или функциональный метод, устанавливает проработку вопросов, связанных с изобретением, кристаллизацией социальных конденсаторов, социально и технически перерожденных организмов, без которых невозможно появление новой архитектуры.

Другими словами, прежде всего — работа **по изучению целевой** установки, по революционизированию самого задания, по конкретизации определенного отрезка новой жизни и конденсации его в наиболее характерных материальных условиях.

Работа эта может быть расчленена на следующие разделы:

I. СОЦИАЛЬНО-БЫТОВЫЕ И ПРОИЗВОДСТВЕННЫЕ ПРЕДПОСЫЛКИ ЗАДАНИЯ ▬▬▬▬▬▬

БАУХАУЗ
АРХИТЕКТОР ВАЛЬТЕР ГРОПИУС

Aleksandr Vesnin, Moisei Ginzburg
(editors), *SA. Sovremennaia
Arkhitektura. Architektur
der Gegenwart. L'architecture
contemporaine*, 6, 1927

40   See *ABC: Beiträge zum Bauen, Het Bouwbedrijf, Izvestiia ASNOVA, Sovremennaia Arkhitektura, Wasmuths Monatshefte für Baukunst*, and Adolf Behne, *Der moderne Zweckbau* (Munich, 1926) and El Lissitzky, *Russland: Die Rekonstruktion der Architektur in der Sowjetunion* (Vienna, 1930).

41   See Christiane Post, *Künstlermuseen: Die russische Avantgarde und ihre Museen für Moderne Kunst* (Berlin, 2012), pp. 81–152; "VKhUTEMAS i Muzei zhivopisnoi kul'tury (MZhK): The VKhUTEMAS and the Museum of Painterly Culture (MZhK)", in *Prostranstvo VKhUTEMAS: Nasledie; Tradicii; Novacii – Space of VKhUTEMAS: Heritage; Traditions; Innovations* (Moscow, 2010), pp. 97–8.

42   See Wassily V. Kandinsky, "Muzei zhivopisnoi kul'tury", *Khudozhestvennaia zhizn* 2 (1920), pp. 18–20; "Thesis of Rodchenko's report on the 'Museum of Artistic Culture'", in Selim O. Khan-Magomedov, *Rodchenko: The Complete Work* (London, 1986), p. 288. Between 1924 and 1928, the MZhK was located in the VKhUTEMAS (or rather VKhUTEIN) building at Rozhdestvenka 11.

43   On VKhUTEIN (Vysshii Gosudarstvennye Khudozhestvenno-Tekhnichskii Institut), see Pavel Novitsky (ed.), *VKhUTEIN: Vysshii Gosudarstvennyi Khudozhestvenno-Tekhnichskii Institut v Moskve* (Moscow, 1929); for a list of the teaching staff at VKhUTEIN, see Khan-Magomedov, *VHUTEMAS*, vol. 1, pp. 245–6.

44   "Die Liquidierung des VChUTEIN, 1930", in Gaßner and Gillen, *Zwischen Revolutionskunst und Sozialistischem Realismus*, pp. 167.

45   See ibid., p. 168.

46   See ibid., pp. 167–8.

47   See Larisa Ivanovna Ivanova-Veén (ed.), *Ot VKhUTEMASa k MARKhI* (Moscow, 2005).

48   Schädlich, "Die Moskauer Höheren künstlerisch-technischen Werkstätten und das Bauhaus", p. 473.

49   Those involved in the exchange included Josef Albers, Erich Borchert, Peer Bücking, Fred Forbat, Moisei Ginzburg, Walter Gropius, Wassily Kandinsky, Nikolai Ladovsky, El Lissitzky, Kazimir Malevich, Hannes Meyer, László Moholy-Nagy, Arkady Mordvinov, Pavel Novitsky, Aleksandr Rodchenko, Lou und Hinnerk Scheper, Arieh Sharon, and Gunta Stölzl.

50   See First Exhibition of Modern Architecture (Pervaia vystavka sovremennoi arkhitektury) in Moscow in 1927; *Sovremennaia Arkhitektura* 4 (1926), p. 108, and the following issues in 1927; *Pervaia vystavka sovremennoi arkhitektury*, exh. cat. (Moscow, 1927); Irina Kokkinaki, "The First Exhibition of Modern Architecture in Moscow, 1927", *Architectural Design* 5/6 (1983), pp. 50–9; K. Paul Zygas, "OSA's 1927 Exhibition of Contemporary Architecture: Russia and the West Meet in Moscow", in Roman and Marquardt, *The Avant-Garde Frontier*, pp. 102–42; Khan-Magomedov, *Konstruktivizm*, pp. 486–88; Tatiana Ephrussi, "Baukhauz na vystavkakh v SSSR 1924–1932", 2012, http://www.actual-art.org; Astrid Volpert, "Bauhaus – umstritten und geschätzt: Zum Wahrnehmungswandel der deutschen Avantgardeschule in Russland", in Hellmut T. Seemann and Thorsten Valk (eds.), *Entwürfe der Moderne: Bauhaus-Ausstellungen 1923–2019* (Göttingen, 2019), pp. 135–6. A reconstruction of the exhibition by Museum MARChI was shown in 2007 at VKhUTEMAS Gallery in Moscow.

51   See *Sovremennaia Arkhitektura* 1928, 1, p. 23; Tatiana Ephrussi, "VKhUTEMAS v Baukhauze: Baukhauz vo VKhUTEMASe: Istoriia dvuch puteshestvii", 2004, http://www.archjournal.ru; Christina Lodder, "The Vkhutemas and the Bauhaus: A Creative Dialog", in *Constructive Strands in Russian Art 1914–1937*, pp. 459–98; Annemarie Jaeggi, "Relations between the Bauhaus and the Russian Avant-garde as Documented in the Collection of the Bauhaus Archive Berlin", in Jörg Haspel et al. (eds.), *The Soviet Heritage and European Modernism*, ICOMOS – Heritage at Risk Special 2006 (Berlin, 2007), pp. 154–7; Ingrid Radewaldt, *Gunta Stölzl: Pionierin der Bauhausweberei* (Wiesbaden, 2018), pp. 132–5.

52   See Khan-Magomedov, *VHUTEMAS*, vol. 1, pp. 247–8.

53   See Larissa A. Zhadova, "Hinnerk Scheper und Boris Ender im Maljarstroj", *Wissenschaftliche Zeitschrift der Hochschule für Architektur und Bauwesen Weimar* 4/5 (1979), pp. 323–7; Renate Scheper, *vom bauhaus geprägt: Hinnerk Scheper; Farbgestalter, Fotograf, Denkmalpfleger* (Bramsche, 2007); Johannes Cramer and Anke Zalivako (eds.), *Das Narkomfin-Kommunehaus in Moskau (1928–2012)* (Petersberg, 2013); Danilo Udovički-Selb (ed.), *Narkomfin: Moscow 1928–1930; Moisej J. Ginzburg, Ignatij F. Milinis* (Tübingen, 2016); see also "H. und L. Scheper: Offener Brief an die Schüler des VChUTEIN, 1930", in Gaßner and Gillen, *Zwischen Revolutionskunst und Sozialistischem Realismus*, pp. 162–3.

(VKhUTEIN)[43] and then dissolved in 1930 "by a decision of the Government Commission".[44] The concept of interdisciplinarity in the avant-garde art school was suspended. A "broad" focus—as the magazine *Press and Revolution* put it—should in future be replaced by a "narrow speciality".[45] The education changed accordingly. The individual faculties at VKhUTEIN were integrated to a certain extent into existing or newly founded universities[46]—the Moscow Architectural Institute (MARKhI) was one of its direct successors.[47] VKhUTEMAS and VKhUTEIN—which pursued "goals that were largely similar to those of the Bauhaus"—"exerted an equally strong influence on the renewal of architecture, product design, and the system of art education".[48] The exchange of ideas between the Bauhaus and VKhUTEMAS and VKhUTEIN and the artistic field was based on personal contacts and correspondence, guest lectures, and participation in exhibitions, excursions, and reciprocal visits by teachers and students, as well as the publication of books and magazine articles.[49] These included the First Exhibition of Modern Architecture,[50] which was organised by the OSA in 1927 at the VKhUTEMAS building; the Bauhaus was well represented. There were also articles about the Bauhaus in the OSA magazine *Contemporary Architecture*, as well as the student exchange in 1927/28 organised with Gunta Stölzl and Arkady Mordvinov,[51] the welcome addresses given by the (di)rectors Hannes Meyer and Pavel Novitsky and the reciprocal invitations they extended to each other in 1929,[52] the collaboration of Hinnerk Scheper and Moisei Ginzburg in the 1930 colour design of the Narkomfin,[53] and, not least, El Lissitzky, who played a key role in mediating the exchange between the art schools and the international avant-gardes.

Faik Tagirov, Design of the book *VKhUTEIN. Vysshi Gosudarstvennyi Khudozhestvenno-Tekhnicheskii Institut v Moskve* (VKhUTEIN: Higher State Art and Technical Institute in Moscow), Moscow, 1929

The Bauhaus in the USA:
Its Reception between the Wars

Margret Kentgens-Craig

Outside Germany, the United States proved to be the most fertile seeding ground for the artistic, intellectual, and educational heritage of the Bauhaus. Here, the dissemination of ideas over the last hundred years has taken place not, as has often been the case in other countries, through the work of individual actors in local niche settings, but through a widespread process with an effect on almost all areas of the practice and teaching of art, design, and architecture. Even if not always identified as such, the assimilation of Bauhaus ideas in America can still be seen today in numerous buildings, works of art, objects, designs, concepts, and educational curricula. This success story has often been traced back to the emigration of artists and architects from Europe, their appointment to influential positions, and their subsequent careers in the USA. In fact, the émigré community there was exceptional in that it included several leading figures from the school. Josef Albers was the first Bauhaus professor to go into exile in the USA. By hiring Albers in 1933, Black Mountain College, a liberal arts school in North Carolina that saw itself as an "experiment in democracy", acquired one of the Bauhaus's most versatile designers and theoreticians. He had helped shape the development of the school in Weimar, Dessau, and Berlin as a student, teacher, and deputy director, and ultimately became the "face of the Bauhaus".[1] In North Carolina, he continued his experiments relating to the nature and behaviours of material and colour. His insights into the relativity of visual perception now seem more important than ever, in our age of "visual overkill". Through Albers, the educational principle of a preliminary course lived on beyond Black Mountain and has a legacy that remains relevant today.

In 1937, Walter Gropius took up his post as director of the Graduate School of Design at Harvard University. One year later, Ludwig Mies van der Rohe arrived in Chicago to head the architecture department at the Armour Institute of Technology, which merged with the Illinois Institute of Technology (IIT) in 1940. This meant that the founding director and lifelong standard-bearer of the Bauhaus, who had coined its name, and the school's third director were both active in America, each of them already recognised as pioneering architects of classical modernism. They were followed by Marcel Breuer, whose innovative tubular steel furniture today is one of the (much-copied) icons of the Bauhaus, and Herbert Bayer, who, together with Breuer, made a significant contribution to the Bauhaus image. As young masters, both played a major role in developing the new profession of "industrial designer". They shared the credit for this with, among others, László Moholy-Nagy: his appointment to the Bauhaus in 1923 marked a turning point in the shift away from a crafts-oriented concept of art toward the unity of art and technology. Like Josef Albers, he was an extraordinarily versatile artist and theoretician. His *Light-Space Modulator*[2] is regarded as the first kinetic sculpture. It was his industrial understanding of design and sense of aesthetics, among other factors, that prompted the Association of Arts and Industries, a regional version of the German *Werkbund*, to appoint him director of the New Bauhaus in Chicago in 1937. The invitation came from Walter Paepcke, chairman of the Container Corporation of America. As a private school, the New Bauhaus needed funding, and Paepcke acted as its sponsor and promoter, while also commissioning Herbert Bayer to plan the ski resort and future cultural centre in Aspen, Colorado. Although a shortage of funds forced the New Bauhaus to close in 1938, it continued the following year as the School of Design, and from 1944 as the Institute of Design, before finally becoming affiliated to IIT. In the early 2000s, the institute was involved in the launch of the Design Thinking movement, and today it runs the only design programme in the USA intended exclusively for graduate studies.

The circle extended further: textile artist Anni Albers accompanied her husband to Black Mountain, followed by Xanti (Alexander) Schawinsky and other members of the Bauhaus, who came as temporary teachers, advisors, or occasional guests. The synergetic effect of networking was also evident in other schools devoted to the Bauhaus, including Mills College in Oakland, California, which had tried, unsuccessfully, to recruit Mies in 1935, and where Moholy-Nagy and Feininger taught

1   Brenda Danilowitz, in Frederick A. Horowitz and Brenda Danilowitz, Josef Albers: *To Open Eyes: The Bauhaus, Black Mountain College and Yale* (London, 2006).

2   Moholy-Nagy worked on this piece from 1922 to 1930, continuing the project beyond his time at the Bauhaus. It is also known as *Light Prop for an Electric Stage*.

the following year. At IIT, Mies was behind the appointments of photographer Walter Peterhans and architect and urban planner Ludwig Hilberseimer.

During World War II, more than thirty Bauhaus émigrés and their families were in the USA. Even if only a few of them are mentioned here, they represent the varied nature of the practice and teaching at the Bauhaus. This was a chance for the Bauhaus to be authentically received in the USA, an opportunity that might perhaps have been realised if the institution had been successfully revived. But the Bauhaus could not be reprised as a school. As much as it was cosmopolitan and internationally oriented, the roots and conditions at its core were too unique to be transferred to other cultural environments. As Mies emphasised, the Bauhaus persisted through the diffusion and further development of its ideas.

If the impact of the Bauhaus in the USA can be traced back to the émigrés and the positions they held, it should not be forgotten that the major influence it had after 1933 would not have been possible without a considerable degree of prior acceptance. This acceptance was shaped in an environment characterised by diversity in language, culture, and politics. Maintaining contacts across the Atlantic meant overcoming considerable hurdles. At the time, travelling by ship was a privilege enjoyed by the few. More than 3,000 nautical miles lie between Bremen and New York alone. All the more remarkable then were the journeys undertaken by the student Werner Drewes, who was one of the first to draw public attention to the Bauhaus in the USA; by his teacher Georg Muche; and by Walter Gropius. These are just some of the many signs that the foundations for receiving the Bauhaus in the USA had already been laid in the interwar years. The unique transatlantic relationship that developed then is key to an understanding of its US reception. Around 1936—i.e. before the first wave of emigration—appreciation of and interest in the Bauhaus resulted from a constant flow of information, finely coordinated marketing, lobbying, and finally an extraordinary congruence of supply and demand: the Bauhaus ideas were on hand in the right place at the right time. The school itself played a significant role in this process. With sophisticated and tireless self-promotion, the

Bauhaus developed a PR model that was ahead of its time, creating a publicity machine that would later become a powerful instrument in the world of professional art and design.[3] German and US architects began exerting an influence on each other even before the turn of the century. Dankmar Adler, who founded the famous Chicago School with Louis Sullivan and others, moved from the Weimar region to America in 1854, when he was still a child. One of Sullivan's grandfathers was himself German. Conversely, the school's achievements inspired Mies's visionary skyscraper designs and provided the context a year later for Walter Gropius and Adolf Meyer's design for the 1922 *Chicago Tribune* competition, the first architectural project by Bauhaus architects in America. The neo-Gothic design that was implemented by New York architects John Mead Howells and Raymond Hood indicates that the time was not yet ripe for them to pit the school's aesthetics and architectural ideas against notions of beauty still dominated by the Beaux-Arts—a concept with which Frank Lloyd Wright also had to contend. However, when Wright came to Berlin in 1910 for the first German exhibition of his drawings at the Academy of Arts, his innovative concepts, which could be seen in the comprehensive, two-volume monograph of his work published by Ernst Wasmuth, were eye-opening for Mies, Gropius, and others from the European avant-garde.

German artists looked with fascination at the USA, with its metropolises, its "American spirit", its elevation of technology to science, and its rationalisation of production and construction. In Berlin, people were raving about jazz and Josephine Baker, who brought the Charleston to Kurfürstendamm. Shortly afterwards, Ise Gropius invited dance teachers from Berlin to Dessau to give the younger Bauhaus teachers an "intensive course" in modern American dance.[4] The Bauhaus band played "Dixieland". Art experts such as Wilhelm Valentiner were working in New York or expressed an interest in opening galleries in conjunction with Ferdinand Möller, Israel Ber Neumann, and others. In late 1920, Walter Gropius introduced regular literary evenings at the Bauhaus, and the American poet Walt Whitman was one of the authors whose work was read there.[5] A striking sign of direct American influence at

the Bauhaus was the appointment early on of the artist Lyonel Feininger as master of form—Feininger had been born and raised in New York. American ideas also reached Weimar on a theoretical level via the writings of educational reformist, philosopher, and psychologist John Dewey.

By the same token, the Bauhaus was gradually being discovered in the USA. In 1924, the German art collector Galka (Emilie Esther) Scheyer began representing the Bauhaus painters Lyonel Feininger, Paul Klee, and Wassily Kandinsky, grouping them together with Alexej Jawlensky under the name "The Blue Four" and showing their work in galleries in New York and Northern CaliforniA. Katherine Sophie Dreier, whose family origins were in Germany, came to acquire works by Paul Klee and Wassily Kandinsky as early as 1922, and in the following years regularly visited the Bauhaus. As a cofounder of the Société Anonyme, she was one of the most influential arbiters of modern art; among other things, she showed the work of 106 contemporary artists from nineteen countries in the exhibition *International Exhibition of Modern Art* at New York's Brooklyn Museum in 1926.

Another important contact was the Austrian architect Richard Neutra, who, like Joseph Urban, Rudolf Schindler, and Frederick Kiesler, had emigrated to America before or shortly after the founding of the Bauhaus and was a proponent of the principles of classical modernism in Southern California. When Neutra came to Dessau as a guest teacher, American exposure to the Bauhaus under Mies was at its height. In the 1930–1932 winter semesters and the 1932 summer semester, more visitors came from the United States than from the rest of the world put together.[6] Mies actively sought to recruit American students and secured a series of enrolments. In the final phase of the Bauhaus, when he ran it as a private school in Berlin, financial pressure caused him to turn to his admirer Philip Johnson for support in raising private funds—a strategy that was almost unknown in Germany at the time. He also entertained the idea of having Johnson as an official representative in the USA: in around 1930, he proposed to him the exciting—though ultimately unrealised—idea of opening a branch of the Bauhaus in New York.[7]

E.L. Fowler, *Tribune Tower*, designed by Raymond Hood and John Howell, Chicago, 1925

3   Margret Kentgens-Craig,
*The Bauhaus and America: First
Contacts 1919–1936* (Cambridge,
2000).

4   Reginal Isaacs, *Walter Gropius.
Der Mensch und sein Werk*
(Berlin, 1983/84).

5   Walter Gropius, letter to
Lily Hildebrandt, Weimar, undated,
late 1920.

6   Ludwig Mies van der Rohe,
journal, Dessau, transferred to
Hans Maria Wingler,
Bauhaus-Archiv Berlin.

PROPHETESS OF "THE BLUE FOUR"

MME. SCHEYER, THE BLUE FOUR AND THEIR ART

"Prophetess of 'The Blue Four'", article on the gallerist Galka Scheyer, 1925

Johnson was probably the most influential of the Bauhaus's supporters in the USA. Together with Alfred H. Barr Jr., director of the newly established Museum of Modern Art, he helped several Bauhaus members to emigrate and devised strategies for making the Bauhaus known to the public. Both Johnson and Barr had had first-hand knowledge of the Dessau Bauhaus since 1929. Mies received his first US commission from Johnson around 1930, namely the design of his Southgate dwelling as an avant-garde "show apartment" and counterpoint to the perception of modernism that was then prevalent in New York. While Mies probably worked on the project with his partner Lilly Reich, he was solely responsible for the interior design of a new, larger apartment on 49th Street in 1932. Accorded a symbolic place in the design was Oskar Schlemmer's famous 1932 painting *Bauhaus Stairway*, which Johnson would pass on to the Museum of Modern Art two years later.[8] Although communication with the USA may have represented only a fraction of the Bauhaus's correspondence, in terms of the results achieved it paints a consistent and informative picture. Walter Gropius's trip to the USA suggests that he went to what was then the "land of unlimited possibilities" in search of more than just adventure and experience. In a letter to Frank Lloyd Wright back in 1925, he had expressed a desire for a face-to-face meeting in the USA.[9] In 1927, he invited Erich Mendelsohn to Dessau to give a lecture on his trip to America.[10] The fact that he was at considerable pains, in the run-up to his own trip in 1928, to make contact with and meet influential representatives of business, industry, the architecture world, and the press in the USA—not to mention his barely veiled self-promotion—points to professional ambitions in America that he might already have harboured.[11] Gropius found himself well accommodated by the attentive journalism in the USA, which reported on the new Bauhaus building and the Weissenhof Estate in Stuttgart. "I returned from America much enriched," he wrote later, "and I truly learned to love this country."[12] In the USA, he witnessed an economic boom, optimism, and a population that could afford to engage with electricity, radio, Hollywood, synthetic fibres, and the task of finding cheap mortgages for construction

Ise Gropius (attributed), Walter Gropius on horseback in front of a wooden shack, Grand Canyon, Arizona, 1928

7   *Deutsche Bauhütte* 13, 24 June 1931. See Christian Schädlich, "Die Beziehungen des Bauhauses zu den USA", *Wissenschaftliche Zeitschrift der Hochschule für Architektur und Bauwesen Weimar* 35.

8   David A. Hanks, "Laboratories of Modernism: The Johnson and Barr Apartments", in D. A. Hanks (ed.), *Partners in Design: Alfred H. Barr Jr. and Philip Johnson* (New York, 2015).

9   Walter Gropius, letter to Frank Lloyd Wright, Dessau, undated (probably summer 1925).

10   Isaacs, *Walter Gropius*.

11   Kentgens-Craig, *The Bauhaus and America*.

12   Walter Gropius, letter to J. B. Neumann, 12 June 1928, Gropius file, Bauhaus Archive Berlin.

projects—while in Germany people were still struggling with the devastating consequences of World War I.

All in all, toward the end of the 1920s there was a marked increase in American interest in the European avant-garde in general and the Bauhaus in particular. This went hand in hand with a striving for modernisation, which henceforth was no longer simply centred on military, economic, and technological concerns, but which also sought a new modernist aesthetic. Mies's visions of high-rise buildings in glass and steel were now reflected not only in the fantastical drawings of architect Hugh Ferriss but also in structures like the Philadelphia Savings Fund Society building by George Howe and William Lescaze, constructed between 1929 and 1932, with an interior designed by Walter Baermann, who was trained in Munich.

In late 1930, George Howe, Buckminster Fuller, and Philip Johnson launched the journal *Shelter*, with articles signalling a rapprochement with modernism. The layout of other journals such as *Architectural Forum* shows a distinct shift toward clear graphics with sans serif fonts. "Pure", "crystalline", "fresh", and "honest" were some of the adjectives used to describe this changing conception of beauty. At the same time, a gap began to emerge between the traditional form of training and the new require-ments of the profession. As interest in the modern international scenes grew in France, the Netherlands, and Germany (with De Stijl, L'Esprit Nouveau, and Neues Bauen) and in Russia with VKhUTEMAS, the Higher Art and Technical Workshops in Moscow, the influence of the Beaux-Arts found itself increasingly on the wane.

Exhibitions also played an important intermediary role in the reception of art. The first Bauhaus exhibition in the USA took place at Harvard University in 1930. Organised by Lincoln Kirstein and his fellow students through the Harvard Society for Contemporary Art, *Bauhaus Weimar Dessau* offered an insight into various aspects of the school. The exhibition later moved on to New York and Chicago. The Bauhaus became much better known in 1932 on the basis of *Modern Architecture: International Exhibition* at the Museum of Modern Art. Along with an accom-panying catalogue and book publication, this exhibition was conceived by curators Philip Johnson and Henry-Russell Hitchcock, under the direction of Alfred H. Barr Jr., as a means to portray Walter Gropius and Ludwig Mies van der Rohe as leading protagonists of the international avant-garde, together with Le Corbusier, J. J. P. Oud, and other exponents of international modernism.

Compounded by major specialist journals such as *Architectural Forum*, *American Architect*, *Pencil Points*, and, above all, *Architectural Record*, there emerged a fragmented, architecture-centred reception. Although Gropius was able to enhance the Bauhaus's profile when he staged the exhibition *Bauhaus 1919–1928* with Ise Gropius and Herbert Bayer at MoMA in 1938, it did not get any closer to providing an authentic understanding of the Bauhaus, with the directorships of Hannes Meyer and Mies omitted from the record. The latter declined the invitation to participate, while Meyer was disregarded in the USA because of his Marxist sympathies.

The opportunity for former Bauhaus architects to realise a building project came in January 1939 when Black Mountain College, at the prompting of Josef Albers, invited Walter Gropius and Marcel Breuer to draw up plans for a new college campus on nearby Lake Eden. The nation, however, was already heading toward a war economy, with rationed building materials and reduced resources. In place of Gropius and Breuer, American architect Lawrence Kocher, the former editor of *Architectural Record*, was awarded the contract in 1940.

During the same period, in 1938, Walter Gropius was finally granted permission to build his own house in Lincoln, Massachusetts: the first manifestation of his architectural philosophy to be realised in his new homeland. This is remark-able because the influence of the Bauhaus was very limited in the USA during World War II and in its immediate aftermath. The anti-German climate often led to feelings of mistrust directed against German immigrants. A number of them, including Gropius, came under FBI surveillance. The reports that emerged from this imply that their "otherness" was observed not only in their language and nationality but also in their architecture. Walter Gropius's "ultra-modern" house in the heart of a traditional New England town fell into this category.

13   Erwin Panofsky, "The History of Art as a Humanistic Discipline", in Theodore M. Green (ed.), *The Meaning of the Humanities: Five Essays* (Princeton, 1940).

14   Wolfgang Pehnt, *Das Ende der Zuversicht: Architektur in diesem Jahrhundert; Ideen – Bauten – Dokumente* (Munich, 1986).

Alfred H. Barr Jr., Philip Johnson, and Margaret Scolari Barr in Cortona, Italy, 1932

Hugh Ferriss, *The Metropolis of Tomorrow*, New York, 1929

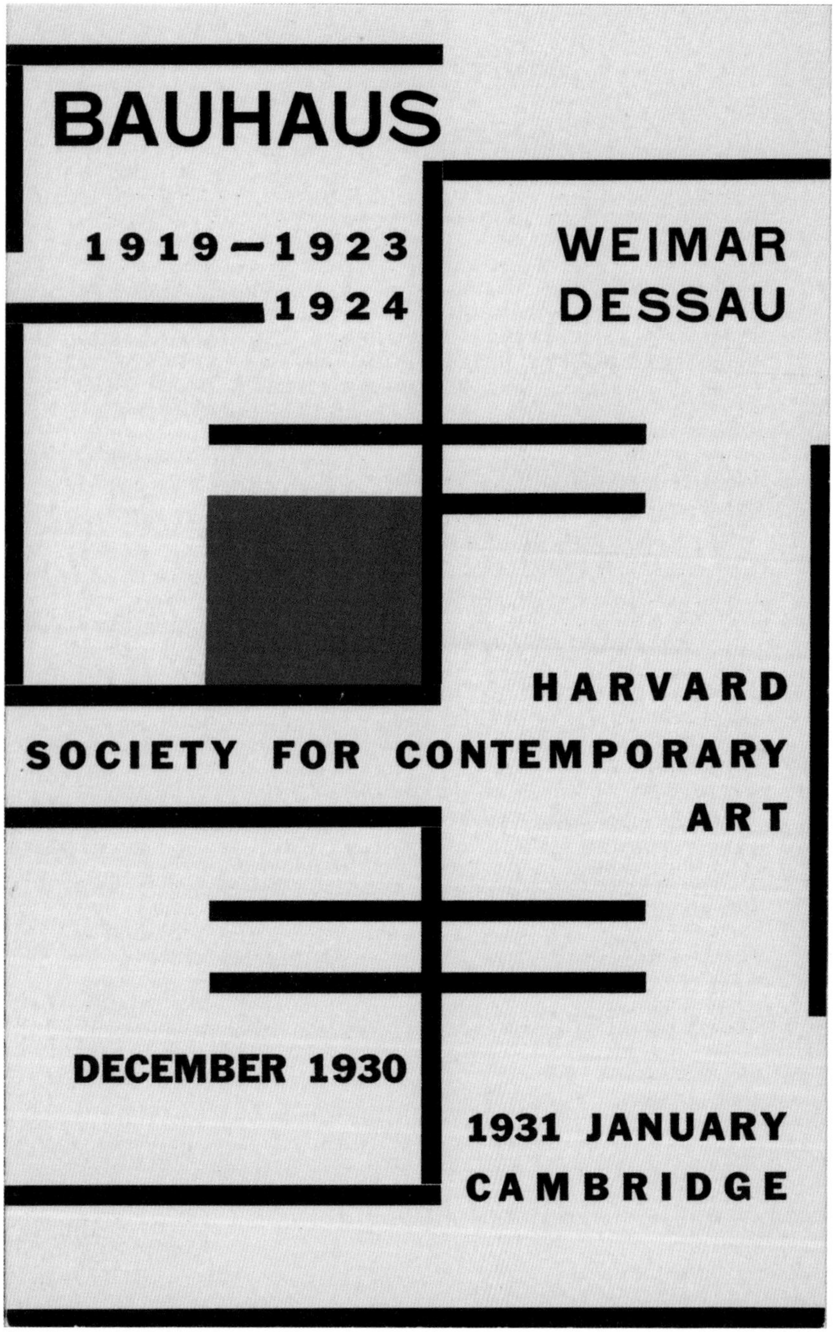

BAUHAUS
1919—1923
1924
WEIMAR
DESSAU

HARVARD
SOCIETY FOR CONTEMPORARY
ART

DECEMBER 1930
1931 JANUARY
CAMBRIDGE

Exhibition catalogue, *Bauhaus Weimar 1919–1923, Dessau 1924*, Harvard Society for Contemporary Art, 12/1930–1/1931

the new bauhaus
AMERICAN SCHOOL of DESIGN
1905 Prairie Avenue
CHICAGO, ILLINOIS
Founded by the
ASSOCIATION of
ARTS and INDUSTRIES

László Moholy-Nagy, Jacket design for the first school prospectus of the New Bauhaus in Chicago, *The New Bauhaus: American School of Design*, 1937

The imputation of Bolshevik-Marxist infiltration, the circumstances of the school's forced closure, and the subsequent emigrations had made the Bauhaus a political metaphor in 1933. Ironically, some of the Bauhaus émigrés affected by this were now suspected of spying for the Third Reich and denounced to the FBI. In the end, these accusations proved to be unfounded. It is quite possible that the individuals who had been targeted never knew that they were under surveillance, because when the Bureau finally closed their files, there were no evident consequences for their careers. By the late 1930s, the Bauhaus had entered a phase in the USA known as "Americanisation", with its protagonists now settled and established and its ideas handed on to a new generation. At this point, however, the reception was no longer simply a matter of cultural transfer, it was also part of the narrative of exile. Erwin Panofsky, perhaps the most influential émigré art historian, commented on the enormous bloodshed that afflicted German culture in the fields of science, philosophy, literature, music, film, art, and art history during the Third Reich and the simultaneous flourishing of creativity in the USA, describing it as "the providential synchronism between the rise of Fascism and Nazism and the spontaneous efflorescence of the history of the arts in the United States".[13] Unlike many of the émigré writers, former members of the Bauhaus did not return to their old homeland after the war, even if not all of them went on to enjoy a successful career in America.[14] Very few of them had been specifically sought out by the USA in the first place, as was the case with Josef Albers, Walter Gropius, and Ludwig Mies van der Rohe, and those who followed them had generally belonged to their inner circle at the Bauhaus.

There can be no doubt that the attempt by the National Socialists to destroy the Bauhaus only led to the revival of its ideas on the other side of the Atlantic. In view of the transmission of these ideas there and further afield, one might wonder what the Bauhaus centenary might have looked like without this phenomenal reception in the USA.

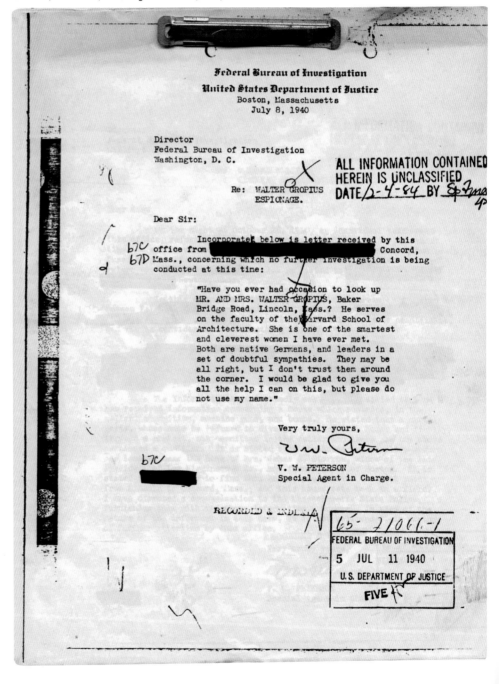

Page from the FBI file on Walter Gropius (Government File, 1940), United States Federal Bureau of Investigation, published in Margret Kentgens-Craig, *The Bauhaus and America: First Contacts, 1919–1936*, Cambridge: MIT Press, 1999, 2000

In Construction—Modernism in Argentina between 1920 and 1930: Protagonists, Programmes, Circles
Silvia Fernández

In the Argentina of the early twentieth century, there was a pronounced contrast between city and country. The immense expanse of the pampas acted as a counterpoint to the key port city of Buenos Aires, which was mushrooming in a disorderly sprawl. The growth of the city and the increase in population density were triggered by a major new wave of immigration, most notably from Europe. The young Argentine government recruited workers from Europe with the help of favourable immigration conditions, the aim being to advance industrialisation, establish businesses, and transform a culture shaped by tradition into an industrialised rural economy built on agri-business and livestock farming.

From 1880 to 1930, Argentina's flourishing economy was largely reliant on trade in agricultural products—for many years the country was regarded as the world's largest exporter of wheat, maize, linen, and meat. Technologies and infrastructures were initially introduced from the industrial powerhouse of Great Britain, with which Argentina maintained close trade relations. But "around 1900, Argentina shifted from importing iron, steam engines, and British railway technology to the production of reinforced concrete, electrification, and the underground rail system known from Germany."[1]

The silos in the ports where grain was stored prior to export became symbols of the Argentine economy. Based on a design by engineer Ernesto Stricker, the Belgian company Bunge & Born[2] constructed the first grain silo in the port of Buenos Aires in 1903–1904 on a "gigantic platform made of reinforced concrete". The silos themselves were "built in brick with an iron frame, an early form of reinforced concrete."[3] The monumental size and specific function of the structure secured it an international reputation and shaped a widespread notion of the pampa in the early twentieth century as a "rural utopia".[4]

In the lecture Walter Gropius gave at the Museum Folkwang in Hagen in 1911 entitled "Monumentale Kunst und Industriebau" (Monumental Art and Industrial Construction),[5] he outlined in some detail his belief that new industrial buildings should be recognised as monumental art owing to their design quality and versatility of application. "Industrial buildings have an inherent sense of originality and might. Their power, severity, and terseness correspond to the organised work that takes place inside them."[6] Among other things, Gropius's lecture showed the silos designed by Ernesto Stricker in the port of Buenos Aires, whose might and size made a vivid impression. Industrial buildings were dedicated solely to function and could thus become the model of a new architecture liberated from historical pressures. It did not matter whether the construction design was applied to a house, an office, or a public building. Another example that Gropius presented in his lecture was the AEG high-voltage factory in the Wedding district of Berlin (1909–1910) designed by Peter Behrens. This design in turn had an impact across the Atlantic: in Argentina, the building for the state oil company, which was founded in 1922, was modelled on the turbine hall. Its engineer, Enrique Mosconi (1877–1946), had studied at the Technical University of Berlin in 1907 and was familiar with Behrens's project first-hand.[7] Like Behrens, Mosconi not only drew up the plans for the industrial facility but also, by designing the firm's communication tools, created a brand, including the company logo. In this way, he crafted AEG's corporate identity as a complete package and raised the profile of the oil industry.

Modernism in Argentina cannot be seen simply as a function of industrialisation. Rather, it was a social process that took place in the cities, an "urban modernity" that had multiple causes, feeding—in Buenos Aires especially—on political, cultural, and economic realignments and a shift in urban planning policy. Between 1916 and 1930, the country turned its back on a long period of conservative politics. The elections produced a social-democratic government that sought both popular sovereignty and the consolidation of democratic values. In these eventful years of turmoil and change, the traditions, behaviours, and socially rehearsed practices propagated under the colonial system—"from the adoption of European architecture to the custom of teatime",[8] as well as ideas about

1   Fabio Grementieri and Claudia Shmidt, *Alemania y Argentina: La cultura moderna de la construcción* (Buenos Aires, 2010).

2   Ibid.

3   Ibid.

4   Beatriz Sarlo, *Una modernidad periférica: Buenos Aires 1920 y 1930, Nueva Visión* (Buenos Aires, 2003).

5   Presented in the Museum Folkwang in Hagen in front of members of the Deutscher Werkbund. The lecture was published in 1913 in the yearbook of the Deutscher Werkbund under the title "Die Entwicklung moderner Industriebaukunst".

6   "Monumentale Kunst und Industriebau", transcription of the typewritten record of Walter Gropius's lecture with the same title from 29 January 1911, in Karin Wilhelm, *Walter Gropius–Industriearchitekt: Schriften zur Architekturgeschichte und Architekturtheorie* (Wiesbaden, 1983), p. 116.

7   Javier De Ponti and Alejandra Gaudio, *Diseño, Identidad y Sentido* (La Plata, 2012).

8   José Luis Romero, *Latinoamérica. Las ciudades y las ideas* (Buenos Aires, 2001).

Korn-Silo derselben Gesellschaft in
Buffalo.

67.

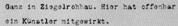

Korn Silo in Südamerika.

68.

Korn-Silo in Buenos Aires.
Ganz in Ziegelrohbau. Hier hat offenbar
ein Künstler mitgewirkt.

69.

Die vorgeführte Bilderreihe macht keinen Anspruch auf
Vollständigkeit, aber vielleicht ist damit (der Beweis erbracht.
dass ein Fabrikgebäude nicht immer ein notwendiges Uebel zu
sein braucht, sondern zum Spiegelbild für die besten Kräfte
unserer Zeit werden kann. Zwar wird eine Stätte der Arbeit nie
in uns so starke seelische Impressionen erwecken können wie
ein Gotteshaus, denn dort werden nur menschliche, keine gött-
lichen Vorgänge verherrlicht, aber in den Bauten der heutigen
Industrie könnte der Keim zu höheren Architekturgedanken ver-
borgen liegen, der sie schon heute der Sphäre der monumenta-
len Kunst näher rückt. Unsere Zeit ist von Problemen erfüllt,

Walter Gropius, Manuscript of his lecture "Monumentale Kunst und Industriebau"
(Monumental Art and Industrial Construction), 1911

Ernesto Stricker, Central warehouse at the port of Buenos Aires, 1903/1904

Pompeu Audivert, *Ciudad*, wood engraving, 1929

"good taste and genteel language"—were ultimately challenged.

Buenos Aires represented a particular demographic phenomenon,[9] as it was characterised by immigrants of extremely diverse cultural, religious, social, and political backgrounds. After the Argentine government's idea of creating a homogeneous society fell apart during the 1920s, the plan was to move toward a "diverse society".[10] It was "a time of uncertain values and a social and ethnic jumble that was also experienced as dangerous, destabilising, and threatening." Buenos Aires in the 1920s was a unique social experiment.

However, it was not only migration but also tourists and people in exile that generated artistic interactions on multiple levels. The luggage they brought to Argentina—in the form of books, magazines, works of art, and above all in the shape of new ideas—was often marked by concepts of European modernism. The capital, Buenos Aires, was transformed into a polyglot city by the influx of people, and many migrant cultures were established in its different neighbourhoods. The question of a new identity arose in conjunction with the culture of the "Criollos", ethnic Spaniards who were born in Argentina, as well as with the indigenous population, whose development in the preceding centuries was just as uneven. This process accelerated in the 1920s, creating a "utopian tension" that brought up questions about traditional values and the future direction of the avant-garde.

These avant-gardes were to be found in circles whose focus might be more narrowly defined or broader in scope. The key actors are presented below. In Buenos Aires the culturally influential magazines *Sur, Martín Fierro*, and the architecture periodical, *Revista de Arquitectura*, produced by the Colegio Central de Arquitectos—and later the magazine *Nuestra Arquitectura* too—became important points of reference and fields of interaction for modernism and its manifold manifestations in art, literature, and architecture. The publisher Victoria Ocampo (1890–1979)[11] played a particularly crucial role here. She brought together designers, authors, and literati; financed visual and textual works; and commissioned architects. The modernist network found in Ocampo its most effective

9   "The number of inhabitants rose from 177,787 in 1869 to 1,575,814 in 1914 and to 1,700,000 in 1919." Fernando Devoto, *Historia de la inmigración en la Argentina* (Buenos Aires, 2003).

10   Sarlo, *Una modernidad periférica*.

11   Victoria Ocampo came from an upper-class family. In 1930, after travelling extensively and engaging with a range of cultural activities, she launched the magazine *Sur*. Four years later, as a committed member of various intellectual, feminist, and antifascist initiatives, she founded the Women's Union of Argentina (Unión de Mujeres de la Argentina, UMA), which was devoted to the struggle for the civil rights of women. She was the only Latin American among the numerous international observers of the 1946 Nuremberg Trials. She received important international awards for her life's work, including the "Order of the British Empire" and an honorary doctorate from Harvard University. In 1977, she became the first woman to be admitted to the Academia Argentina de Letras, the leading institution for the cultivation of the Spanish language in Argentina.

Víctor Delhez, *Hélice* (Propellers), black-and-white photograph, 1931, published in the magazine *Sur* 2, 1931

Man Ray, *Victoria Ocampo*, Paris, 1922

mouthpiece: her focus was consistently trained on the cultural transfer between Europe and Latin America. In 1931, she founded the magazine *Sur*, a literary cultural journal that was a key point of reference for intellectual circles in Argentina, until it was discontinued in 1970. The modern approach of the magazine was most evident in the design of the cover page, which Ocampo was responsible for from the start. The white, empty space served not only as a background but also as a dynamic design field. The symbol of the arrow pointing downwards was a characteristic motif that also appeared in the work of the painter Xul Solar. The founding manifesto of *Martín Fierro* also called for a modernism that was rooted in the culture of the southern hemisphere while at the same time integrating European thought—without, however, reproducing it uncritically. This was evident in the choice of title, *Martín Fierro*: Fierro was a literary figure from a poem of the same name by José Hernández. In this national epic, Fierro represented the gaucho, who came into conflict with both the indigenous population and the big landowners. His person combined various cultural influences, which were ultimately deployed against Europeanisation, and was indispensable as an art-theoretical platform. In a 1924 article in *Martín Fierro*,[13] one of the magazine's co-founders, Xul Solar (1887–1963),[12] discussed the work of his colleague Emilio Pettoruti (1887–1971)[14]: "Despite all the confusion, there is a clear tendency toward simplicity of means; clear, solid architecture; and pure sculptural form, which preserves and accentuates the abstract meaning of line, material, and colour, while preserving the absolute freedom of expression and composition."[15] The focus on artistic means, the reduction to basic forms, and the importance of a free form of art that wants to depict nothing more than itself, are ideas that are also central to Solar's work. He had studied at the Munich Kunstwerkstätten (art workshops) from 1921 to 1924, where he was influenced by the work of the Bauhaus: Paul Klee was "the European artist Xul Solar most admired, one whose attitude to painting, music, and spirituality Solar followed and shared."[16]

Pompeu Audivert (1900–1977) was a Catalan artist who came to Buenos Aires as a child. His work, which was published in magazines,

also provides early evidence of the Argentine avant-garde. According to art historian Guillermo David, his 1929 woodcut *Ciudad* represented a "merging of the ideas of Futurism, Bauhaus, and German Impressionism. It is a pivotal work in the history of printmaking, engraving and, beyond that, of Argentine art as a whole. It features intense chiaroscuro effects. The view out of the window, a motif drawn from European art history, shows an assembly of cubic structures in a staggered array next to one other. The buildings are clearly accentuated by hatching, while at the same time serving as abstract symbols.

The photographer and artist Víctor Delhez (1902–1985) was of Belgian origin and emigrated to Buenos Aires in 1926. In addition to his work with woodcuts, which he showed in solo exhibitions from 1929 on, he gained a reputation as a photographer. His experimental approach became a model for many local artists in Buenos Aires. In abstract compositions, he emphasised the materiality, surfaces, and textures of the objects he photographed. The sheen of a polished metallic surface, reflections, and fragmented pictorial spaces became characteristic features of his photographs. This brought him both artistic and economic success, with the result that he received numerous commissions from the Argentine establishment—including for the design of interiors—and finally made the grade as a staffer for the avant-garde magazine *Sur*.

In 1922, the young Argentine architects Alberto Prebisch (1899–1970), Ernesto Vautier (1899–1982), and Alejo Martínez Jr. visited France, Germany, and Italy. After his return Martínez lived in Concordia, Entre Ríos, and in 1925 designed the the house of Dr Péndola Díaz, a radical modern town house. Over the next seven years he built twenty avant-garde houses, expressing a clear commitment to a style of functionalist architecture that became a landmark of the city.

Martín Fierro published an article in 1925 entitled "Ciudado con la Arquitectura" on Prebisch's and Vautier's works. The project "Cuidad Azucarera", for the densely populated province of Tucumán in the northwest of the country, was presented as a new idea in urban planning and architecture, where the chaos of the rapidly growing city was combined with housing that was socially appealing and had

12   Xul Solar was closely associated with the members of the literary group known as the Martinfierristas, which included Jorge Luis Borges among others.

13   *Martín Fierro* 1, nos. 10–11 (1924).

14   Emilio Pettoruti studied painting and drawing in Argentina and won a scholarship in 1913 to study art in Florence, where he first came into contact with futurist artists prior to becoming associated with cubism. His collaboration with Xul Solar, whom he had met in 1916, led to Argentina's first artistic avant-garde.

15   Sarlo, *Una modernidad periférica*.

16   Mario Gradowczyk, *Xul Solar* (Buenos Aires, 1994).

17   Sarlo, *Una modernidad periférica*.

Alberto Prebisch, Home of Luis María
Campos, ground floor, Belgrano,
Buenos Aires, 1931

Alberto Prebisch, Home of Luis María Campos, ground floor, Belgrano, Buenos Aires, 1931

an attractive design. Although the magazine did not have a clearly political orientation, this highlighted architecture as a field of social activity.

The architect Wladimiro Acosta (1900–1962) had a particularly strong impact in Buenos Aires in the 1930s, developing a synthetic form of Neues Bauen architecture that took into account the requirements of a tropical climate. Born in Odessa, Acosta emigrated to Argentina in 1928. He had initially studied in Berlin and come into contact with expressionism via Erich Mendelsohn, with whom he was acquainted, and later with Bauhaus rationalism and its approach to design, with Walter Gropius as its chief exponent. In Buenos Aires, he first worked in Alberto Prebisch's architecture firm. From 1932 on, Acosta used the Helios system he had devised, which was conceived both for residential housing and as a module for urban planning.

Also important in this context are the architects Rocha and Enrique Martínez Castro. Their seminal country house *El Destino* was erected in 1929—a prime example of Bauhaus-style rationalist architecture and quite unlike the historicist buildings typical of this period in Argentina.

The architect and engineer Antonio Vilar (1889–1966) was also an exponent of geometric sparsity, the flat roof, and a rational approach to layout. He systematically applied his design objectives to the construction of the Argentine People's Bank and worked together with Willi Ludewig on the building of the Argentine automobile club ACA and the hospital in Churruca. The so-called Hindú Sports Club, which he designed in 1932, consisted of a gym, basketball court, halls, and an outdoor swimming pool. Vilar made skilful use of the structure of interlocking cubes, setting the top-lit gymnasium farthest back. He then ran a long, three-storey walkway through the middle of the site that was open on both sides and functioned as a grandstand. From here the spectators could see the court from one side and the swimming pool from the other.

In this context, Victoria Ocampo once again played a key role as an architectural catalyst: in 1927 she had a modern house by the sea built that she had designed herself. It was "a plain, unfussy house: just a few cubes. [...] I was hungry for white walls without stucco

Invitation to the exhibition, *Fotos,
Horacio Coppola y Grete Stern,*
at the headquarters of *Sur,*
March 1935

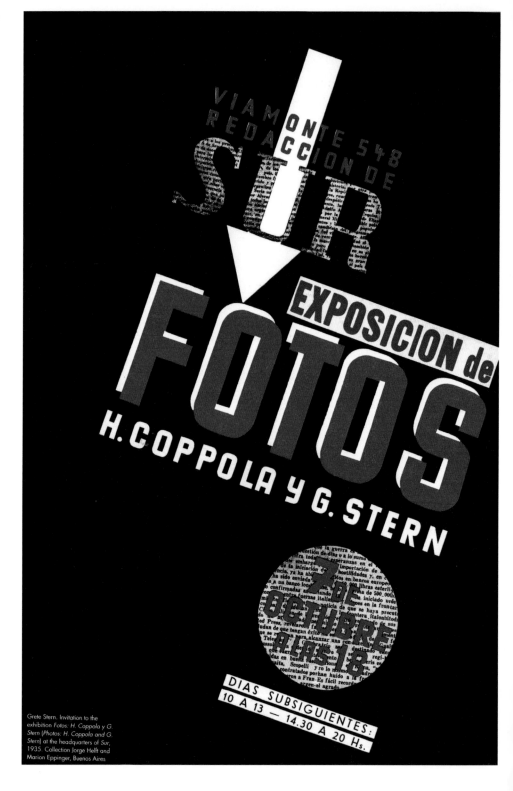

Wladimiro Acosta, sketch of the project *City Block*, 1931

mouldings and other decorations," as she later said of this building. Shortly afterwards she commissioned Alejandro Bustillo (1889–1982) to build another house, this time in the capital, Buenos Aires: "I loved the house in Rufino de Elizalde more than any other. I admired it as an architectural work. I loved its spaces and wanted to fill them with small numbers of beautiful things. Nothing superfluous or mindless. I was fascinated by modern architecture. It represented a new way of living." Ocampo put her contacts and enthusiasm at the service of architecture as a "new way of living".

Ocampo had first made Gropius's acquaintance in 1929 in Berlin, and they met again in 1934 in Rome, then in London, in Cambridge, MA, and in Buenos Aires in 1968, when Gropius visited the city in the context of the project jointly run by Amancio Williams for the German Embassy, although this was ultimately not realised. Ocampo included Gropius's article on "Total Theatre" in the first edition of the magazine *Sur*. Based on his relationship with Ocampo, Gropius established a studio in Buenos Aires between 1931 and 1934, in conjunction with the architect Franz Möller, who was an integral part of his Berlin studio. Möller settled in the city, although the major projects they were anticipating—the housing complex in Puerto Nuevo and a barrio in the seaside resort of Chapadmalal—failed to materialise. However, they did build two family homes in Florida, in the province of Buenos Aires that had an influence on Wladimiro Acosta, Antonio Vilar, and Alberto Prebisch. Moreover, working on a smaller scale, the Gropius-Möller studio made domestic furniture, launching on the market different types of metal furniture, whose exclusive designs were manufactured in Argentina.

There is a direct connection between the Bauhaus and Buenos Aires through Horacio Coppola (1906–2012), Grete Stern (1904–1999), and Josef Tokayer (1911–1972), all of whom quickly connected with the network of artists in Buenos Aires. Coppola, who had attended the photography classes run by Walter Peterhans at the Bauhaus, emigrated to Buenos Aires in 1935 with his wife Grete Stern, another Bauhaus student. At Ocampo's prompting, they mounted an exhibition in the same year on the *Sur* premises. They had Wladimiro Acosta design a house outside the city and it was here that Buenos Aires's intellectual elite gathered in the 1940s. Stern and Coppola's commitment to the reception and dissemination of Bauhaus aesthetics in the fields of photography, graphic design, and the visual arts influenced an entire generation of Argentine artists.

Josef "José" Tokayer was born in Germany but went on to become a pioneering figure in the Argentine art, photography, and design scene. He studied at the Bauhaus in Dessau, completing his training in graphic design in 1931. Between 1933 and 1936, Tokayer lived in Paris, where he ran a photography and advertising agency. After an interim period in Hungary, he returned to Germany. In 1937, in view of the growing threat posed by National Socialism, he finally emigrated via Marseille to Buenos Aires, where he worked as a graphic designer for Argentine publishing houses, printing firms, and pharmaceutical companies. According to critic Sigwart Blum, Tokayer was "the only Bauhäusler working in Argentina who designed modernist graphics".

Argentine modernism, and the irrevocable changes that went with it,[17] was manifested above all in a new mindset among the intellectual elite, a mindset that was influenced by Europeans but was able to establish itself on a firm footing in its own right. At the end of the 1940s, this multifaceted process was to be taken up again by a young generation of artists and creatives who once again examined and questioned the utopia of modernity, thus accelerating its advance even further.

Horacio Coppola, *Toldos* (Awnings), gelatin silver print, 1931

Mexican Modernism Meets the Bauhaus
Enrique Xavier de Anda Alanís

Any discussion of the intellectual influence the Bauhaus had in Mexico must also take into account the context and conditions there that provided fertile ground for its ideas. In the early 1920s, Mexico and Germany were reeling from the devastating effects of wars from which they were both slow to recover. Even though the underlying circumstances that led to World War I in Germany and the civil strife in Mexico were completely different, they were responsible for profound shifts and realignments in society, art, and politics in both countries. The Mexican Revolution broke out in 1910, and its effects continued to reverberate into the 1920s. The uprising against the president and dictator Porfirio Díaz was the beginning of a series of skirmishes and riots, some of them extremely bloody, that spread across large parts of Mexico. The revolution was waged by very different sociopolitical groups, who not only fought out their conflicting interests but also, to some extent, actuated a social revolution. This was spearheaded by the army of Emiliano Zapata. The main outcomes of the protracted struggles of the Mexican Revolution were the violent political ouster of the established Mexican oligarchy, the reshaping of the Porfirist state apparatus, and the dismantling of Porfirio Díaz's army, which had been structured like the German army. This was accompanied by the rise of a new ruling class, emerging from the ranks of various revolutionary (*caudillo*) movements, and the establishment of new state structures. The pressure for social reform had been one of the main triggers for the revolution in 1910, but important changes were only implemented from 1917 on when the Federal Mexican Constitution was written and in the periods of presidential rule that followed under Alvaro Obregón, Plutarco Elías Calles, Lázaro Cárdenas, and Manuel Ávila Camacho.

In 1925, the young Mexican architects Juan Legarreta (1902–1934) and Juan O'Gorman (1905–1982) began to engage with European architectural journals such as *Moderne Bauformen: Monatshefte für Architektur und Raumkunst* and the writings of Le Corbusier (*Towards a New Architecture*), and to implement the main features of functionalist and rationalist architecture in their work. Legarreta and O'Gorman played a prominent part in introducing functionalism to Mexico, along with architects like José Villagrán García, Enrique Yáñez, and Luis Barragán.

Legarreta was primarily interested in housing construction—which had become a more pressing concern as Mexico City became increasingly urbanised—subsumed into a functional unit but also allowing communication with the space outside because the buildings face onto the street. In 1932, a private construction company headed by Carlos Obregón Santacilia announced a competition for the design of small workers' flats and houses entitled "La casa obrera mínima" (the basic worker's house). Legarreta won first prize and with it the opportunity to build 120 standardised houses in the Balbuena district. He presented three different models comprising 54.9, 44.1, and 66.6 square metres respectively. With the agreement of Enrique Yáñez and Augusto Pérez Palacios, who came second and third in the competition, the designs for these models incorporated certain elements from their projects. The houses were designed in such a way that they ran from east to west or vice versa, with their floor plan and location determined by their orientation to the sun, light, and air. They constitute an interesting urban figure, which Legarreta also implemented in the San Jacinta and La Vaquita housing estates. The individual elements of the houses were staggered and characterised by projections and recesses, creating courtyards that offered both privacy and shade. Inside the complex, the blocks were designed exclusively for pedestrians and formed public spaces, while outside they were connected to streets with cars and traffic.

In the same period, O'Gorman had been commissioned to construct a number of school buildings. Among his most famous designs, however, were the artist's houses he created, which were a local variant of rationalism. In 1932, O'Gorman built a studio and residence for the painters Diego Rivera and Frida Kahlo—both structures became icons of the "new architecture" in Mexico. The house's glazed curtain wall opens up the space, with the supply of light regulated by a sawtooth roof. The building's façade includes deep blue and strident tones. Next to it is the first of the

Juan Legarreta, Workers' housing, Mexico City, c.1932

Juan Legarreta, Workers' housing, Mexico City, 1932

three projects, the studio house that O'Gorman had designed for his father, who was also a painter, a building intended for five residents. The cubic body of the house is two storeys high, with the ground floor heavily recessed and the upper floor appearing to float above it. The structure is supported by steel columns, with concrete slabs used for the ceilings and walls. The result is a fully glazed curtain wall whose windows can be folded and pushed to the side.

In 1933, Legarreta and O'Gorman delivered a series of panel discussions on the subject "Is Functionalism Architecture?" to members of the Association of Mexican Architects. In these discussions, they decried the prevailing school of thought, instead promoting a functionalism that was tailored to Mexican needs. This ultimately caused the Academy of Fine Arts to split: one camp consisted of supporters of historicism and traditional decorative art, while the other comprised a few architects who, with Legarreta and O'Gorman at the forefront, sought to connect to the European avant-garde. Legarreta decided not to attend the congress and instead sent a letter condemning the teachers of the old academic tradition. In his speech to the congress, O'Gorman explicitly argued the merits of modernist architecture with its possibilities of universal application: "Ladies and gentlemen, I am convinced that the true and only feasible architecture of our time is one that seeks to satisfy clear material needs. These are fundamental needs common to all people. Respectable technical architecture, a true expression of life, and at the same time architecture as a scientific instrument of modern-day humanity! [...] No one has yet come up with the idea of building different means of transport for Mexico and France, for instance. The international architectural style bears witness to the global orientation of scientific education. Ignoring this architectural style is like trying to hold back the tide with a broom. [...] This type of architecture is criticised on the grounds that it is in the business of building boxes. You will excuse me if I ask you, is a book shaped like a prism or a box? And does it have any objections to this shape? Of course not, because this is the form best suited to its production and use. The book's box-like shape is what is international—

regardless of whether it is French, German, or Mexican, red or green, large or small."

Any analysis of the encounter between the Bauhaus and Mexico must include mention of the second Bauhaus director, Hannes Meyer. He emigrated to Mexico in 1938 and lived there with his family until 1949, at which point he moved back to Switzerland, where he finally settled until his death. In Mexico, Meyer initially intended to engage with the socialist revolution. Architects José Luis Cuevas and Enrique Yáñez acted as intermediaries, gaining Meyer access to the Mexican architectural scene. Although they were generally well informed about the Bauhaus themselves, they offered Meyer a forum in which he could play a comprehensive role in the architectural discourse. This initially took the form of articles for specialised journals and lectures at the school of architecture, accompanied by the founding of a planning institute headed by Meyer. In 1938, he presented his recommendations for how architects should be trained in Mexico in a lecture at the Academia de San Carlos, home to the School of Architecture:

Architecture, like all the arts, is a matter of public morality. The architect fulfils an ethical function by analysing his architectural work with a relentless passion and love for the truth and executing it valiantly as an act of creation. The call for an "international architecture" in an age of national autarkies, when colonial peoples are awakening, Latin America is standing together against the clutches of imperialist and reactionary foreign capital, and socialist construction is in progress in the Soviet Union, in an age in which the railways, large land holdings, and oil wells are being expropriated for the benefit of the people of Mexico—this call is the expression of a snobbish vision cherished by those architectural aesthetes who dream of a standardised world of glass, concrete, and steel, detached from social reality [...]
Take, for example, the architectural situation in the Soviet Union, where at present more than eighty national cultures, liberated from tsarism, are not only developing their own literature and art but

also producing more than eighty architectures with a national character. This is a civic understanding that is socialist! And this leads us to the problem of content and form in architectural art. This architectural form must have social content, otherwise it becomes pure decoration […]. If we espouse the architectural view outlined above, we can draw the following conclusions, more or less, with regard to the training of the architect: […]

The pervasion of socio-economic reality demands of him a sociological understanding (without him becoming a specialist in sociology in the process!). For how can he work in Mexico, for example, where all kinds of social systems intersect (pre-feudal, feudal, and capitalist, as well as a transitional system that is changing over to socialism)? How is the architect to understand the forms of housing pertaining to these four social stages? […]

In conclusion, let me summarise the suggestions for reorganising your architecture academy:

1. Introduce productive education in the realities of building.

2. Develop the system of work brigades.

3. Foster the relationship to the public and to social criticism.

4. Liberate students and professors on the economic level.

5. No class-based education for intellectuals! No artistry!

Meyer finally began working for the government authorities in 1942, at which point he came into contact with prominent figures in the "new architecture" movement, including Ignacio García Téllez, a politician who worked closely with President General Lázaro Cárdenas, sharing his basic approach to the socialist restructuring of society. In the same year, Meyer designed the Lomas de Becerra public housing complex. His design envisaged the construction of large residential blocks based on the maxims of the CIAM (Congrès Internationaux d'Architecture Moderne) and

the prototype of the balcony-access houses he had created in Dessau-Törten in 1929. Meyer's project did not come to fruition, however, and the Lomas de Becerra estate was not built until 1956, when it was constructed on the basis of Mario Pani's design. It is my opinion that the most important influence that Meyer's thinking had on Mexican architecture was the spatial planning concept that he implemented between 1944 and 1946 at the building department of the IMSS Mexican Social Security Institute, headed by Ignacio García Téllez.

While many myths have grown up around the impact Hannes Meyer had in Mexico, the influence of the work of Michel van Beuren (1911–2004) can be clearly traced. From 1931 to 1932 he had studied at the Bauhaus in Berlin under its last director, Ludwig Mies van der Rohe. Van Beuren was not only a pioneer but also a catalyst for the introduction of modernist design in Mexico in the 1930s and 1940s. He finally settled in Mexico in 1936 but gained more recognition for his furniture design than for his architectural work. In Mexico, he found both suitable materials and workers steeped in a centuries-old tradition of craftsmanship. The modernist architecture scene had given rise to plain cubic houses, built by the architects mentioned that followed the ideas of the European "Modern Movement"; now the open, light-flooded rooms were to be furnished as well—with chairs and sofas, beds, tables, and cupboards, which were to be distinct from traditional furniture. Shortly after his arrival, van Beuren contacted a number of Mexican designers and architects who advocated modern design and interior decoration, among them Clara Porset (1895–1981). She had approached Gropius seeking admission to the Bauhaus, but he had advised her instead to study at Black Mountain College with Josef Albers, as the Bauhaus had come under political scrutiny. In 1944, she and van Beuren applied for a prize announced by the Museum of Modern Art in New York and, together with other Latin American designers, they represented Latin America's avant-garde tendencies in furniture design at MoMA. They showed bentwood armchairs and loungers, whose seats consisted of broad strips of plaited webbing. In the 1950s, van Beuren's furniture combined

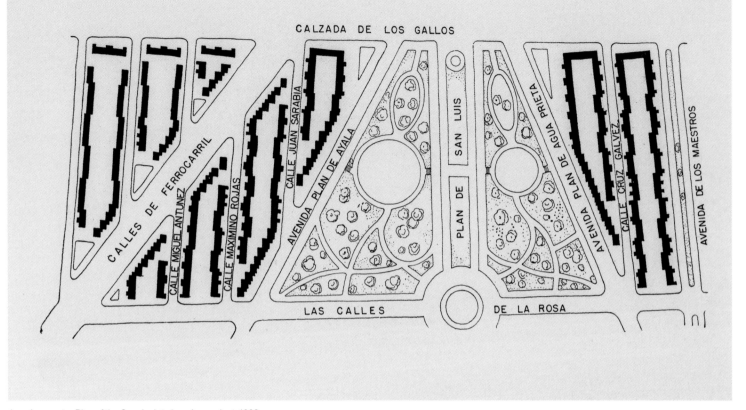

Juan Legarreta, Plan of the San Jacinto housing project, 1932

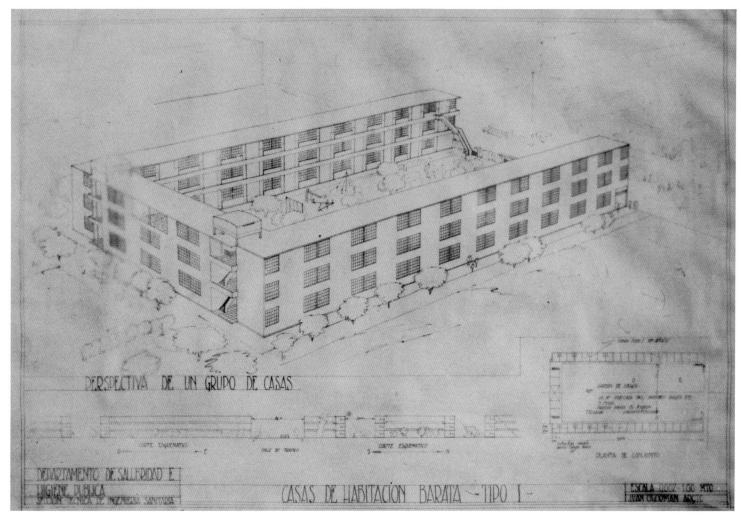

PERSPECTIVA DE UN GRUPO DE CASAS

CORTE ESQUEMATICO — E   CALLE DE TRAFICO   CORTE ESQUEMATICO — N

PLANTA DE CONJUNTO

DEPARTAMENTO DE SALUBRIDAD E. | ESCALA 0.002 : 1.00 MTO.
HIGIENE PUBLICA   CASAS DE HABITACION BARATA — TIPO I —   JUAN O'GORMAN ARQ'TO.
SECCION TECNICA DE INGENIERIA SANITARIA

Juan O'Gorman, Design for a community house, c.1930

Juan O'Gorman, Studio building of
Diego Rivera and Frida Kahlo, Mexico City, 1931

Juan Legarreta, Workers' housing,
type 3, Mexico City, 1934

Michel van Beuren, Interior with armchair with bentwood runners and plaited webbing, 1950s

Students in the architecture faculty and participants in Mathias Goeritz's
Basic Design course, 1949

the ergonomic principles learned at the Bauhaus with local high-grade woods and textiles, thereby creating his own unmistakable style, which became highly prized. Although he was not a member of the Bauhaus himself, Mathias Goeritz (1915–1990) had always had close ties with the artistic and architectural avant-garde, and he had a particular intellectual affinity with Paul Klee. During a period spent in Spain, where among other things he founded the School of Altamira, Goeritz was appointed professor at the School of Architecture in the city of Guadalajara. Soon after his arrival in Mexico in 1949, Goeritz took part in discussions about nationalism in the art of the Mexican Revolution—whose proponents included Diego Rivera and other painters—and the avant-garde tendencies coming from Europe that were supported by Goeritz. Inspired by the Bauhaus preliminary course, which had been introduced by Johannes Itten and continued by László Moholy-Nagy, Goeritz started out by running the course Introduction to the basic design course in Guadalajara and later at the Universidad Iberoamericana (1954–1959) and the Universidad Nacional Autónoma de México (UNAM). There he geared his teaching to techniques that Itten and Moholy-Nagy had promoted at the Bauhaus, inculcating skills designed to foster imagination, the development of craftsmanship, and the free handling of materials. In summary, we can say that the spirit of the Bauhaus, as taught in the laboratories of Mathias Goeritz's preliminary course, played a key part in educating an entire generation of Mexican architects between 1950 and 1980.

I would like to conclude by demonstrating the process of knowledge transfer, which can be traced from the avant-garde through to the second half of the twentieth century, evident in the work of Gabriel Chávez de la Mora (b. 1929). He studied with Goeritz in Guadalajara and had taken part in his basic design course, which, as Chávez de la Mora now admits, had a decisive influence on his career as an architect. Brother Gabriel, who today lives in a monastery as a Benedictine monk, designed the chapel belonging to the Santa María de la Resurrección monastery in Ahuacatitlán in 1957, in the process redesigning the liturgical furnishings, long before the Second Vatican

Council in 1964 called for the congregation and the liturgical centre to be connected. Founded in 1956 by Brother Gabriel in the spirit of the Bauhaus, the Emmaus workshops in the monastery produced numerous wooden and silver objects designed and manufactured by the monks themselves, as well as textiles and paintings, all of which contributed to the dissemination of a new formal language that was identified with modernism in Mexico for decades. The fact that Brother Gabriel is still active as an architect and also runs the arts and crafts workshop in the Tepeyac monastery indicates that the spirit of the Bauhaus is alive and well in Mexico.

Performance in the Museo Experimental El Eco, sculpture designed by Mathias Goeritz, Mexico City, 1952/1953

Vernacular Modernism: Carlos Isamitt and the Founding of the New School of Fine Arts in Chile, 1928

David Maulen and Valérie Hammerbacher

In the new political climate that followed World War I, the countries of Latin America experienced an unprecedented surge in development. A comprehensive programme of reform led to the emergence of a liberation movement focusing on cultural identity, nation-statehood, and an independent self-image. The hegemonic powers had lost influence, thus creating new opportunities for action on the domestic front. Although the Chilean state had been nominally independent of the Spanish crown since 1810, it was still dominated, economically speaking, by the leading industrial nations of Great Britain and, subsequently, the USA.[1] Chile's colonial history, which had determined the country's position as part of the Spanish Viceroyalty of Peru since the mid-sixteenth century, had not only been instrumental in shaping its economy, politics, and society up to this point, but was also particularly evident in the education system. The first training centres for artistic design to be founded in Chile were the Academy of Painting (Academia de Pintura) and the School of Arts and Crafts (Escuela de Artes y Oficios), both of which had been opened in Santiago de Chile in 1849, based on a European model. The intellectual creativity expressed in painting and sculpture at the academies of fine arts was juxtaposed with the manual craftsmanship required in applied arts. The two were linked to one other in a hierarchical relationship. They not only represented different areas of the visual arts, but were also defined by a strict segregation of creative work. The artist and educational reformer Carlos Isamitt problematised this split in the 1920s. As a writer and campaigner for changes in educational policy, Isamitt was adamant that folk art, which had previously been marginalised, could also be integrated by connecting the two areas. If the visual culture of craftsmanship in Chile's indigenous communities could be put on an equal footing in the cultural narrative, this would help the country to free itself from its colonial legacy. A unique mode of expression could be achieved by drawing on the discrete forms and patterns of Chile's various indigenous communities.

Isamitt's activities are part of a movement that began in the late 1910s. When the Chilean Workers' Federation (FOCH) was founded in 1919, it played a key role in modernising the educational establishment's curricula and objectives. Acting in tandem with the group of primary-school teachers known as *normalistas*,[2] it played a crucial role, from 1920 to 1924 in particular, in reorienting pedagogic and didactic methodologies: it was guided by the principle that education is the engine of social change, not only formulating but also producing conditions for creative, political, and social activity. One of the most important achievements of this movement was the creation of a network of self-governing schools, which also offered classes in technology. The process of industrial modernisation in Chile was to be supported by the school curriculum and adapted to the needs of a society in the industrial age. These schools represented an alternative to state and private educational institutions, most of which were cast in the Catholic mould. The mission of the primary-school teachers' movement incorporated the reformist approaches of influential educational theorists in Europe: the teachings of Johann Heinrich Pestalozzi and Friedrich Fröbel, who included stimulating children's games in their kindergarten concept, had just as much impact as Maria Montessori's idea of the child as the "builder of his or her own self". Georg Kerschensteiner's attention studies were integrated, along with Jean-Ovide Decroly's overhaul of "frontal" instruction and the ideas for early education propounded by reformers José Vasconcelos, José Ingenieros, Carlos Vaz Ferreira, and José Carlos Mariátegui in Mexico, Argentina, Uruguay, and Peru respectively.[3]

In 1924, the artist, composer, and musicologist Carlos Isamitt was asked by the *normalistas* association to study the teaching concepts of the arts and crafts schools and develop a new pedagogic model. Isamitt's research during his time at art school had been conducted in direct contact with indigenous communities, and he was able to draw on knowledge of pre-Hispanic culture from groups in Chile in the mid-1920s. In 1918 at the latest, he had begun the theoretical and practical study of the geometric design principles of indigenous art, analysing and

1 The governments of Paraguay and Chile had attempted to nationalise natural resources and use the revenue to develop homegrown industry, but their efforts were nipped in the bud at the urging of Great Britain and its local allies.

2 Primary-school teachers who were trained not at universities but at teaching colleges.

3 Another figure worth mentioning in this context is the abstract painter Julio Ortiz de Zárate. As a member of the Montparnasse group, Ortiz de Zárate had also taken an active part in the constituent assembly of March 1925, where he pushed for educational reform. In 1927, he put a draft reform before the government, which proposed transforming the fine arts academy into a school of applied arts with teaching facilities in different parts of Santiago.

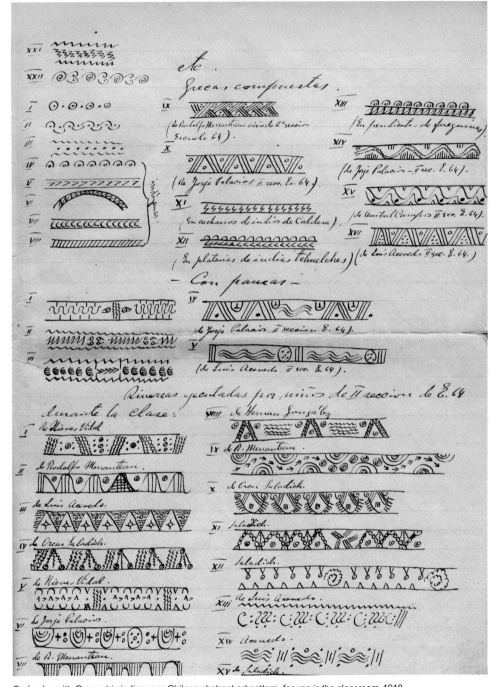

Carlos Isamitt, Geometric indigenous Chilean abstract art pattern, for use in the classroom, 1918

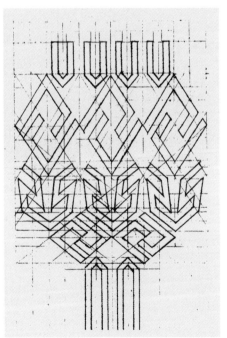

Beatriz Danitz, Geometrisation of a thistle, Gestalt analysis in the textbook for the New School of Art, 1928

Johannes Itten, "Vor mir steht eine Distel" (I Have A Thistle Before Me) in Bruno Adler (ed.), *Utopia. Dokumente der Wirklichkeit*, Weimar, 1921

systematising the images and assessing the possible application of these principles in the new methodology for teaching art. Of particular note here are the didactic experiments he conducted both in the extreme south of the country and on the island of Chiloé. The results of these experiments constitute the most important link between Isamitt's ideas for teaching art and the manifestations of the European avant-garde he had got to know during a trip in 1925. He visited the world's fair in Paris and studied the various pedagogical approaches in Europe and the Soviet Union. Isamitt analysed 300 school timetables and was particularly impressed by the VKhUTEMAS arts and crafts school in Moscow, the colour theories of Karol Homolacs, the Polish schools, and, above all, the art courses offered by the reform schools in Germany and Austria.

As European correspondent for the Chilean newspaper *El Mercurio*, he summed up his findings as follows:

"There is a school in Moscow that combines all the arts into industrial art. The Moscow school of fine arts and the school of applied arts, which have now merged, are full of innovative spirit. In preparation for their studies in architecture, painting, or sculpture, the students must take a preliminary course in which they acquire a basic knowledge of colour, volume, and space. This course teaches the elementary principles of different materials, spatial distribution, and volume formation."

In 1928, Carlos Isamitt finally succeeded in pushing through a radical reform of the system of higher education in the arts.[4] In January of that year, immediately after the government decrees passed by Chile's president General Carlos Ibáñez del Campo came into force, Isamitt was appointed director of the Escuela de Bellas Artes in Santiago de Chile. The college, which had previously been part of the university's philosophy faculty, was now put under the control of the Ministry of Education. This enabled Isamitt to establish his concept in two key locations: he integrated the school of applied arts, which was now called Escuela de Artes Aplicadas, into the school of fine arts, and developed a preliminary course for the students that enriched the new methods of the European avant-garde with influences derived from the country's indigenous communities.

The *primer año de prueba* was key to the structure of the curriculum. This "probationary year" was compulsory for all students. During this year, Gestalt psychological analyses were carried out, the distribution of masses in the image studied, and the relative strengths of figurations measured. Analysis of works from art history was also on the curriculum. Figures from Michelangelo's fresco *The Last Judgement* in the Sistine Chapel were broken down into triangles to reveal the structure of the painting and the rules governing it. Isamitt called for practice sessions focusing on physical substance and texture, as well as an exploration of the materials and creative work with the properties of plaster, metal, and textiles. By studying the contrasts between soft and rough, light and dark, the students developed an understanding of the particular material. The individual lessons were rooted in testing and experimentation. As in the preliminary course that Johannes Itten had introduced at the Bauhaus in Weimar in 1921, and which he ran until 1923, Isamitt combined elements of Gestalt psychology with an analysis of geometric forms. A motif that Itten presented to his students for them to work on artistically also appeared in Isamitt's exercises—the image of a thistle that was to be developed as a drawing. While Itten had his class work with the rubric "I experience a thistle"—asking them to investigate their individual emotional investment in the object rather than depict the visual image of the plant as the creative expression of a perception—Isamitt dismantled the motif, breaking it down into a pattern of geometric forms. The thistle was used as the starting point for analytical drawing and separated out into stalk, leaves, and flower. The drawing was then dissected into oblique angles and finally rendered in abstract, planar form.

In this way, typical geometrical forms from Andean culture were turned into course content and acknowledged for the first time as having cultural value. This geometrisation takes its cue from the crosses, stair-like motifs, steps, and triangles in the literature on Andean cultures in the 1920s. They can be found in the textbook *Dibujos indígenas de Chile* (Indigenous Drawing in Chile), produced by Abel Gutiérrez and José Dvoredsky, who did the cover illustrations. It was published in 1929 with the subtitle *Para estudiantes, profesores y arquitectos, que quieran poner en sus trabajos el sello de las culturas indígenas de América* (For students, teachers, and architects who want to put the seal of indigenous American cultures on their work). On the back of the book, José Dvoredsky showed the letters of the alphabet, each with lines in the form of a staircase. In the picture section there is often a *chakana*, the "Andean cross", attributed to the cultures of the Aymara and Mapuche, who were settled in today's northern and southern Chile respectively. It was also a common symbol in the highlands of Bolivia and Peru, dating back to the Incas. The four directions symbolise the four cardinal points of the Incan Empire. The reference to the Mapuche culture, however, reveals another dimension. On the one hand, this culture provides an abundance of forms and allows modernist art to be connected with concepts of abstraction; on the other hand, it has a special significance in Chilean history. The word "Mapuche" is composed of two sub-elements, *mapu* (earth) and *che* (man). The Mapuche were divided into various regional identities, such as the Picunche (Men of the North), the Wilhiche (Men of the South), the Ldafkenche (Men of the Sea), the Wenteche (Men of the Valleys) and the Pewenche (Men of the Monkey-Puzzle Tree), who constitute the largest and best-known group. The Picunche, the people of the north, had already been conquered by the Incas in pre-Columbian times, although the structures of the territory remained intact. The Mapuche (or, more precisely, the Pewenche and some of the Wilhiche) resisted Spanish rule, engaging in a fierce and—unlike with most other indigenous communities in America—successful struggle against colonisers for over 300 years. From the mid-sixteenth century onwards, the Mapuche established their own state—partly based on the Spanish model—which endured until 1883. Their art thus represented a culture of anti-colonial resistance that was able to vigorously assert itself and became, for Carlos Isamitt, the reference point for a history of Chile that was new and at the same time traditional.

Most of the conservative-minded press were strongly critical of the school reforms and spoke of a "dictatorship of cubism and futurism". With

4 A lively exchange of views took place between Mexican and Chilean representatives and theorists from the reform movement. In 1922, Minister of Education José Vasconcelos brought Gabriela Mistral, the Chilean teacher and future winner of the Nobel Prize for Literature, to Mexico.

5 "The works of a people must come from the ranks of the people." In the original Spanish quotation, Isamitt uses the word *raza*. Quoted in Teresa Navarro's PhD dissertation, *Carlos Isamitt*, Universidad de Chile, Santiago de Chile, 1957, n.p.

Los Tejidos Araucanos como base
para una
Arquitectura Típica Nacional.

Quien conozca los huacos y toda la variedad de dibujos de los diversos tejidos araucanos, no nos podrá negar que en ellos tenemos la base para lograr un tipo propio de línea arquitectónica.

Si pensamos que la intensificación del sentimiento americanista nos encamina a las fuentes mismas aborígenes, para obtener de ellas la precisa orientación, encontramos que nada nos puede ofrecer mayores posibilidades que los dibujos simples, de planos estilizados hasta la ingenuidad armoniosa, de los viejos huacos y de los trarihues o fajas y demás tejidos y choapinos mapuches.

Si bien es cierto que en los más antiguos tachos de barro cocido, está a la vista la influencia de la cultura de los aimaraes y quechuas y en ella a su vez la de los chilchas y mayas, no podemos negar que hay una línea y una ideología personalísima, que por sobre el tiempo y el duro batallar por la tierra y por la vida, se ha conservado en los tejidos mapuches y en la misma alfarería hayta hoy.

Bastaría tener a la vista algunos ejemplares para comprobar la enorme riqueza decorativa, fácilmente aprovechable en la concepción de una arquitectura típica nacional, que darían un maravilloso carácter y colorido a nuestras ciudades.

Si bien es cierto que en ellos predomina como en todos los motivos aztecas y egipcios, la línea quebrada que parece emparentarlas y aproximarlas, no deja de ser interesante la enormidad de combinaciones graciosas que es posible admirar. En los trarihues, por ejemplo, donde los motivos más bellos distribuyen grecas y figuras de una armoniosa composición que dicen claramente del sentimiento estético innato en estas viejas razas de América.

Su espíritu contemplativo, manifestado en el dibujo de sus tejidos, va estilizando la observación simplista, escuela de la propia naturaleza, que hacen del araucano, un valioso elemento que aporta con ingenuidad conciente impresiones sintéticas de gran utilidad, para arribar a una total complementación decorativa y formar motivos arquitectónicos interesantísimos.

En "El Alcázar de las Perlas", de Abul Beka, hallamos al genial arquitecto inspirándose súbitamente en la fantástica visión del crepúsculo en la montaña nevada para lograr la belleza increíble del alcázar de la Alhambra de Granada. Poseemos arquitectos artistas que pueden encontrar en la alta y singular cordillera andina y en la estupenda visión de nuestras montañas, inspiración. Si a esa bellísima visión de cumbres, torreones de granito matizados por crepúsculos únicos, le agregamos las estilizaciones posibles recogidas por los indígenas y reveladas en sus tejidos y huacos, algún día podremos mostrar al mundo orgullosos, lo que salvará el tiempo, representando la verdadera arquitectura chilena, con sabor, colorido y valor propios, dando carácter a nuestras ciudades y fortaleciendo con la enseñanza visual, el amor a la incomparable belleza de Chile.

C. C. N.

Faja o trarihue.

"The Araucanian tissues as a basis for a National Typical Architecture", in *Arquitectura y Arte Decorativo*, 6/7, 1929

Marcial Lema.–Composición decorativa.

Marcial Lema, Work in black-and-white, published in the magazine of the school of applied arts, 1928

no attention paid to the fact that the connection between people of different ethnic origins had been a central feature of Chilean culture since the sixteenth century, the advocates of reform were accused of having adopted the art of "less developed peoples" in the curricula of the country's most important art school. But even if Isamitt took the diversity of Chilean culture into consideration, the auspices under which he evaluated cultural production are ultimately problematic. In accordance with the state ideology of Carlos Ibáñez del Campo's government, he advocated a nationalistic glorification of Chilean history, which codifies the cultural identity of the population based on origin and ancestry.[5]

In October 1928, the process of educational reform was brought to an abrupt end, even as the reform syllabi remained in effect at the Escuela de Bellas Artes until its closure in 1929. Although the new school of fine arts only represented a brief episode, its influence in terms of discourse and action persisted in various places. In 1946, for example, Tibor Weiner revisited the concept of a comprehensive pedagogy that would include all areas of design in his model of *Arquitectura Integral*, or integral architecture—but now under different auspices.

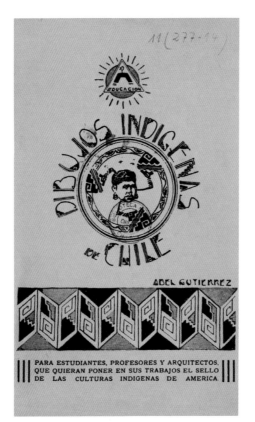
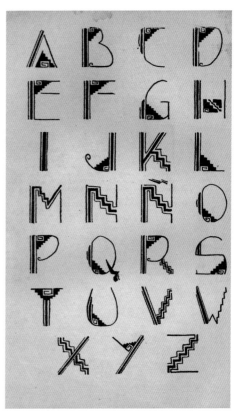

José Dvoredsky, Illustrations in the handbook *Dibujos indígenas de Chile* by Abel Gutiérrez, 1928

Breaking the Wave—From the Bauhaus to Mohamed Melehi and from the Casablanca School to Nassim Azarzar
Salma Lahlou

Mohamed Melehi (b. 1936) is a painter, photographer, graphic designer, sculptor, teacher, and activist. He trained in northern Morocco, then in Spain, Italy, and the USA. In 1964, he returned to Morocco, enriched by a wealth of experience and engagement with an aesthetic discourse anchored in the contact he had had with the Bauhaus teachers who had brought German modernism to the USA. His experience as a teacher in Minneapolis, his stay in New York, and his knowledge of the works of Ludwig Mies van der Rohe, László Moholy-Nagy, Herbert Bayer, and Josef Albers helped forge his interest in the teaching methods and various types of artistic works discussed at the Bauhaus, while also familiarising him with different, intersecting artistic practices. Drawing on the basic principles of the Bauhaus, one of Melehi's key concerns was to question the hierarchy between the arts, as set down in the founding manifesto of the Bauhaus in 1919 and then vividly expressed in the merger of the School of Arts and Crafts and the Academy of Arts in Weimar. He challenged the boundaries between genres and the strict separation of the applied and fine arts in order to create a new aesthetic concept that gave design and form a significance beyond religious or bourgeois iconography.

Nassim Azarzar (b. 1989) is a visual artist and graphic designer. A graduate of the École supérieure d'Art et de Design d'Orléans in France, he settled in Morocco in 2013. Together with Guillaume de Ubéda, he founded Atelier Superplus, a studio for experimental graphic design. In 2016, he cofounded Think Tangier, a platform for exploring the intense urbanisation of the city through projects that combine research, design, and art. In 2018, he was one of the founders of Atelier Kissaria in Tangier, whose focus is on experimental, artisanal printing techniques. Since 2018, he has been working on *Bonne route*, a collaborative project focused on the ornamentation used to decorate Moroccan lorries. Taking as his starting point the aesthetics of popular culture, Azarzar uses a contemporary visual language that is rooted in the local setting.

Melehi and Azarzar are separated by two generations of artists, yet explore the vernacular language and abundance of design in Moroccan culture and its conceptualisation in the field of contemporary aesthetics. What does it mean today for a contemporary artist to translate Melehi's work into a personal reading? What remains of the aesthetic problematics raised by Melehi and the Casablanca School? And how has Azarzar enriched his own artistic practice?

Melehi and I have been meeting regularly since 2016, when I curated the exhibition *The Casablanca School of Fine Arts: The Making of Art and History with Belkahia, Chabâa and Melehi* at the sixth Marrakech Biennale.[1] This exhibition was the starting point of my research on the artistic practices that have crossed Morocco throughout the twentieth century and the epistemological issues they brought forward. Just under a year later, I presented an exhibition in Germany entitled *In the Carpet*,[2] which included Melehi's painting *New York, 1963*. Here we see a flat surface designed with three primary colours—blue, red, and yellow—delimited by three types of lines: straight, curved, and wavy. The lines create three two-dimensional visual spaces. A Zemmour carpet (the work of a Berber tribe in the Central Atlas Mountains dating from the 1940s) hung on an adjacent wall as an extension of the painting. These two objects created a reference field of forms and colours, whose similarity would have been evident to both the layperson and the connoisseur. This dialogue between folk art and high culture is Melehi's key focus and constitutes one of the two major pedagogical undertakings of the Casablanca School of Fine Arts (the "Casablanca School").

Founded in the early 1920s on the initiative of the French colonial authorities and officially inaugurated in 1951, the Casablanca School underwent a renewal in 1964 spurred by a group of artists and researchers who brought together artistic and social reform as a joint project. The conceptual and artistic contribution of the Casablanca School had two goals: first, to expand the social relevance of the artist and of art in the context of building a democratic culture, as both are indispensable aspects

1   The exhibition ran from 24 February to 8 May 2016 at the sixth Marrakech Biennale, *Quoi de neuf là – Not New Now*–chief curator: Reem Fadda; collaborating curators: Fatima-Zahra Lakrissa and Salma Lahlou. There were online catalogues that could be downloaded as PDFs but these are no longer available.

2   *In the Carpet* – Über den Teppich, Institut für Auslandsbeziehungen, Stuttgart, 28 October – 18 December 2016; Berlin, 13 January – 12 March 2017; collaborating curators: Salma Lahlou, Mouna Mekouar, and Alya Sebti.

3   See online catalogues (no longer available) for the sixth Marrakech Biennale (see n. 1).

4   It was during this short period that the most prolific exchanges took place among the teaching staff, whose work was at its most striking and compelling.

5   This carpet appeared on the cover of the first edition of *Maghreb Art* produced by the Casablanca School of Fine Arts in 1965.

6   Bert Flint, "La dynamique de l'art du tissage au Maroc", in *Tapis et tissages ruraux marocains: Teresa Lanceta*, exh. cat. Villa des Arts, Fondation ONA (Casablanca, 2000), pp. 5–10. See also Bert Flint, *La Culture afro-berbère de tradition néolithique saharienne en Afrique du Nord et dans les pays du Sahel* (Marrakech, 2018).

Nassim Azarzar, "Digital Studies
no. 1: Patterns and Colors",
after Mohamed Melehi, 2019

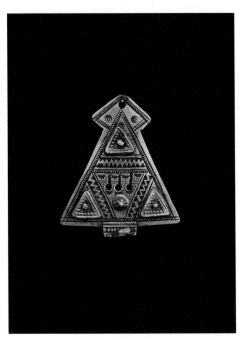

Fibula, Berber jewellery, photographed by Mohamed Melehi, 1965

of decolonisation and catalysts for cultural change; the idea was to explore and re-appropriate the country's collective heritage in order to make it culturally productive. The second objective was to use the artistic discourse to help develop the principles of Moroccan modernism.[3]

Between 1964 and 1969,[4] a new team formed the nucleus of what came to be known as the "Casablanca School", under the leadership of the artist Farid Belkahia (1934–2014), who was appointed director of the school from 1962 to 1974. Melehi headed the workshop for painting, sculpture, and photography. He replaced the Greco-Roman sculptures, which had served as models, with a traditional Moroccan carpet.[5] This radical gesture brought to light a new paradigm: the necessity of passing on a vernacular formal language to students of fine arts. He reiterated this in front of another audience in the context of his exhibition at the Bab Errouah gallery in Rabat in 1965, following a comment by a journalist who had classified and dismissed his painting as American. Here he set out to establish a connection between his painting and popular Moroccan art. Toni Maraini (b. 1941), an art historian and anthropologist, offered a general introductory course on Moroccan art history, a narrative that broke with historical and cultural continuums as well as with the principle of separating different artistic genres. Bert Flint (b. 1931), a linguist and passionate researcher of folk art and rural traditions, shared his ideas about the material culture of the rural population with the students at the Casablanca School and made a lifelong commitment to the study of jewellery, carpets, and weaving. His aim was to unlock the inherent qualities of these forms of art, unconstrained by the Eurocentric criteria determining visual culture.[6] The School's team expanded to include Mohamed Chabâa (1935–2013), who took over the workshop for decoration, graphic art, and calligraphy. As head of the workshop, Chabâa's influence on the syncretic alliance of architecture, art, and crafts was of crucial importance.[7]

The teaching team's research work was carried out in the workshops and appeared in *Maghreb Art*, a publication devoted to traditional, rural, and urban works of art, which came out in 1965, 1966, and 1969. The third

7   Nadia Chabaâ, "Chabaâ's Concept of the '3 As'", bauhaus imaginista, accessed 26 July 2019, http://www.bauhaus-imaginista.org/articles/2430/chabaa-s-concept-of-the-3-as/fr.

8   *Maghreb Art* 3 (1969), pp. 7–8.

9   Magdalena Droste, *Bauhaus: 1919–1933; Reform and Avant-Garde* (Cologne, 2016), p. 10.

10   Mohamed Melehi, interview with the author, Casablanca, February 2019.

11   "Together with Abdellatif Laâbi and Mustapha Nissaboury, he worked on the magazine *Souffles* (1966–1971), for which he designed the lettering and cover: a black circle bleeding through its circumference into a subtle pointillist blur. The title is in French with Latin letters based on the Kufic script, one of the oldest calligraphic forms of Arabic writing." Quoted from a text by Fatima-Zahra Lakrissa and Salma Lahlou, in *Melehi: 60 ans de création, 60 ans d'innovation*, published in conjunction with the retrospective exhibition at Espace Expressions CDG, Fondation CDG, 21 March – 30 April 2019, Rabat, p. 29.

and final issue represented the culmination of the process that had developed in the first two editions, in which the group's research questions had been brought to light, identified, defined, classified, and mapped out. Melehi created a formal synthesis of applied and fine art through the analysis of the pictorial traditions of the mosques and zawiyas (religious and educational institutions) of the Souss region. Paintings on wooden surfaces (ceilings and doors) and walls were examined for their artistic significance. As he explained it, these juxtapositions "are an expression of the will, of a conscious decision, of the freedom to choose and create, a rational process that manifests in the geography of the surface, treated by numerous formal studies, by an execution in movement. It is the expression of an idea characterised by a striving for clarity, for a universally valid composition alternating graphic elements and forms [...] a style of painting [that is] consistent with the preoccupations of contemporary art."[8] Melehi's ideas picked up on the principles of the Bauhaus: the connection between "art and technology" as a depiction of the zeitgeist.[9] Here, Melehi posed questions similar to those that had been raised by the European reformist movement in the field of decorative and applied art. But he explicitly turned his back on the mechanistic worldview of the European debate, which was influenced by industrialisation, and took his cue from art historian Alois Riegl's concept of *Kunstwollen*, which art historian Ernst Gombrich described as "artistic volition", based on the operation of unconscious principles and impulses inherent to any creative work. This led to a transcultural encounter with Western concepts, which were applied—but not before being redefined—to the complex question of Moroccan modernism. By referring to the Bauhaus, it was possible to gain a new perspective on a centuries-old artistic heritage. For Melehi, "the Bauhaus was instrumental within this process, as this modernism was primarily concerned with people and giving creative shape to their lives. The preoccupation with *Kunstwollen*, which found expression in form and design, enabled Moroccan art to develop as an autonomous, universal art that combined form, function, colour, and beauty."[10] Melehi's formal approach—enriched by his

Mohamed Melehi, Wall painting, Hôtel Les Roses du Dadès, Kelâa M'Gouna, 1971–1972

left: Mohamed Melehi, *Soleil oblique*, cellulose paint on wood, 1970

12   The following artists took part in this exhibition: Mohamed Ataallah, Farid Belkahia, Mohamed Chabâa, Mustapha Hafid, Mohamed Hamidi, and Mohamed Melehi.

13   Mohamed Melehi and Mohamed Benaissa—both of whom were born in Asilah, a small port town in northern Morocco—launched the Cultural Moussem of Asilah, an annual cultural festival, in 1978.

reflections on Morocco's visual and artistic tradition—allowed him to develop a visual polysemy based on the undulating line of a curve or wave. This universal archetype was the key pictogram Melehi used to produce meanings associated with natural forces like earth, air, fire, and water as they are contingent on spatial and compositional structure.

As Melehi's artistic work continued to evolve, he also developed cultural initiatives in which different practices could come together. In his view, if you wanted to change something in society, it was necessary to create a dynamic relationship between art and other spheres of life and ensure that the work reached a broader audience. He designed the avant-garde magazine *Souffles* (1966–1971)[11] and published *Intégral* (1971–1978), a journal he had founded with Toni Maraini and ran together with her. It is also important to remember the historical exhibition on Jamaa El Fna Square in Marrakech in 1969[12] and the Cultural Moussem of Asilah arts festival in 1978.[13] An art that goes out on the street sets out to "integrate", not "decorate", public space. With this in mind, Melehi collaborated on six architectural projects with Farid Belkahia, Mohamed Chabâa, and the architectural firm Faraoui and de Mazières.[14]

My research on the processes of transmission and transcription that Melehi carried out with his students and on Azarzar's modus operandi highlights four steps that are crucial to the creation of work that is autonomous and effective: observation, deconstruction, experimentation, and formulation. Azarzar's procedure can be compared to the visual, artistic research that Melehi and Chabâa carried out in the workshop for decoration, calligraphy, painting, and photography at the Casablanca School. It is their work—viewed as if looking through a prism—that constitutes the starting point for the artistic language through which various objects are perceived. When the students' drawings were published in the third issue of *Maghreb Art* in 1969, Melehi clarified his methodological approach: "We start from a legacy that offers more possibilities than anything acquired through academic and classical means to end up with avant-garde shapes and patterns."[15] This view marked a shift from "traditional" form to modern design, thereby creating new regimes of representation and

14 The Holiday Club in M'Diq (1968–1969), the Hôtel Les Gorges du Dadès in Boumalne Dadès (1970–1971), the Hôtel Les Roses du Dadès in Kelaa M'Gouna (1971–1972), the Hôtel Les Almoravides in Marrakech (1970–1972), a hotel in Taliouine (1971–1972), and the Faculty of Medicine in Rabat (1972–1978). Maud Houssais, "Archives du Cabinet Faraoui et de Mazières", bauhaus imaginista, accessed March 2019, http://www.bauhaus-imaginista.org/articles/3886/archives-du-cabinet-faraoui-et-de-mazieres.

15 *Maghreb Art* 3 (see n. 8), pp. 31–44.

Painted ceiling of a mosque in South Morocco, detail,
photographed by Mohamed Melehi, 1969

concepts that have their origin in major elements of the visual structure—the wave, spiral, square, triangle, red, black, yellow, etc. Following this methodology, I asked Nassim Azarzar to venture a contemporary reception of Mohamed Melehi's language of forms and colours. Azarzar explains, "I created an experimental set-up with basic elements, and then found new visual content by combining these elements in various ways, allowing something different to emerge, while retaining a connection to the original."[16]

Based on this narrative, which illustrates the relationship between transmission, continuity, and the transcription of forms, Azarzar had several options open to him: Should he retain Melehi's wavy line and stick to a formalist approach? Or should he foreground Melehi's work and establish a dialogue with his take on local and contemporary culture? Should he allow the two zones of enquiry to intersect? The two artists come together in their efforts to create an art of the present, to invent an autonomous and effective language, to produce an image that simultaneously reveals its contextual and contemporary character as well as its original form. An art, in other words, that reconciles two concepts that theoretically seem at odds: "the idea of the 'avant-garde' (which aligns the present with the future and transfers it into contemporary life), and the idea of 'tradition' (which explains the present by looking at the past and finds its reflection in time-honoured values)."[17]

16   Nassim Azarzar, interview with the author, Rabat, June 2019.

17   Toni Maraini, "Situation de la peinture marocaine", *Souffles* 7/8 (1967), pp. 15–16.

Designing and Coding
Peter Weibel

1   Ernst Mach, *Beiträge zur Analyse der Empfindungen* (Jena, 1886).

2   Christian von Ehrenfels, "Über Gestaltqualitäten", in *Vierteljahrs-schrift für wissenschaftliche Philosophie*, Leipzig 14/1890, pp. 249–92.

3   Hans Robert Jauss (ed.), *Die nicht mehr schönen Künste. Grenzphänomene des Ästhetischen* (Munich, 1968).

4   Wassily Kandinsky, *Point and Line to Plane: Contribution to the Analysis of the Pictorial Elements.* First published as Bauhaus Book, vol. 9, 1926.

5   Walter Gropius, "The Theory and Organisation of the Bauhaus", in Herbert Bayer, Walter Gropius and Ise Gropius, eds., *Bauhaus 1919–1928* (New York: Museum of Modern Art, 1938). Available here: https://www.moma.org/documents/momacatalogue_2735_300190238.pdf. First published as *Idee und Aufbau des staatlichen Bauhauses* (Munich: Bauhausverlag, 1923).

6   In Hans Eichner (ed.), Friedrich Schlegel, *Kritische Ausgabe* (Paderborn–Munich–Vienna, 1967) vol. 2, pp. 182–3.

7   De Stijl, *Zur neuen Weltgestaltung*, vol. 4, 1921/8, pp. 124–5, in *De Stijl*, part 2, 1921–1932, reprint (Amsterdam—Den Haag, 1968), pp. 100–1.

8   Piet Mondrian, *Neue Gestaltung. Neoplastizismus. Nieuwe Beelding*, Bauhausbuch vol. 5 (Munich, 1925).

The modern concept of design has its origins in the nineteenth century. In his book *Analysis of Sensations* (1886), Ernst Mach provides the basis of a design theory,[1] which was then further formulated by Christian von Ehrenfels in *On Gestalt Qualities* (1890).[2] In the 1920s, this led to a German school of Gestalt theory (Max Wertheimer, Wolfgang Köhler, Kurt Koffka, Kurt Lewin), and at the same time the concept of Gestalt or design became widespread in the field of art.

Far-reaching changes after the First World War led to a whole generation radically searching for a new order. This included an aesthetic revolution that can be identified in the changing names for art institutions: prior to 1900, art universities were called Academies of Fine Arts (*Akademien der schönen Künste*), but thereafter just Academies of Arts (*Akademien der Künste*), as the "no longer fine arts" (Hans Robert Jauss, 1968)[3] came to the fore in the twentieth century. How did this come about? On the one hand, the elements of painting were subjected to scrutiny. Painting's means of depiction—the point, the line, the plane—were formerly used to create representations of real objects, but now they themselves became the subject of painting.[4] This self-representation of the means of representation led to abstract painting, which had a strong following at the Bauhaus with Johannes Itten, Wassily Kandinsky, and Paul Klee. The world of objects was also seen to represent itself in objects, and also in ready-mades by Marcel Duchamp. A third direction—which was specifically developed in, at, and around the Bauhaus—attempted to overcome the gulf between the figurative and the abstract by postulating universal principles of design for use in both two-dimensional and three-dimensional forms.

The founder-director of the Bauhaus, Walter Gropius, was striving for the remedy of total design: "This dawning recognition of the essential oneness of all things and their appear-ances endows creative effort with a funda-mental inner meaning. No longer can anything exist in isolation. We perceive every form as the embodiment of an idea, every piece of work as a manifestation of our innermost selves."[5]

This faith in the power of design as a positive force in the world is characteristic of the move-ment of the Bauhaus school. By introducing the term "design", the Bauhaus distanced itself in both theory and practice from the concept of aesthetics. The Bauhaus school stood for a historical break with art's aspirations to represent reality. "Universal principles of design" were introduced, which could be implemented functionally in all the genres, whether painting and sculpture or the crafts and architecture. The design principles for a plane, a two-dimensional work were the same as those for a room, and vice versa. Paintings, objects for everyday use, and buildings all followed the same visual patterns of line and colour. The Bauhaus set a new guiding principle against the imperative of the Romantic school: instead of "the world must be made poetic", the Bauhaus said that "the world must be designed!" "Progressive universal poetry" (Friedrich Schlegel, Athenäum Fragment no. 116, 1798)[6] was replaced by "universal principles of design". The tone was set in the De Stijl manifesto of 1921, *Towards a Newly Shaped World*,[7] followed by a number of Bauhaus publications: *New Design* (Piet Mondrian, Bauhaus Book, vol. 5)[8] and *Basic Concepts of New Design Art* (Theo van Doesburg, Bauhaus Book, vol. 6)[9]. In the course of the twentieth century, no new "Art Academies" were founded; the new art institutions in Germany instead decided to call themselves Universities of Design (*Hochschule für Gestaltung*), while in the English-speaking world they were Institutes of Design. Alongside the broad claims made by artists and designers to use design to change society and improve everyday life, there were also sceptical voices. In his essay "gestaltung?" (1928), painter, architect, and designer Naum Gabo criticised the increasing use of the word: "to this day i fail to understand for what reason and with what justification this word has so rapidly become established in our circles, so that it will soon have a greater significance in modern art theory than the word 'art' itself. People speak and write solely of 'design,' and are ashamed to mention art with its full name—instead it is denoted just with a chaste 'a'."[10] In various manifestos, the following aspects were particularly emphasised: 1. The concept of "design" reflects a new unity of art and technology. This led to the term "aesthetics" being replaced by "design" and "style" by "form". 2. Although the manifestos had different focuses, they all shared a claim to the universality of the concept of design. Theo van Doesburg wrote: "A single element suffices for form, e.g. the square. The line both separates and combines, it gives the work direction and force. Composition is not the highest goal. The highest goal is the transition to a universal form of design."[11] Piet Mondrian's view of design that bears an essence of the universal was based on the basic geometrical shapes of the square, the triangle, and the circle. Inspired by Kasimir Malevich's 1915 visual manifesto *Black Square*, set against a white background, Mondrian introduced the style of "neoplasticism" in 1920, also known as "new design".

At the Bauhaus, these new principles were taught in all the workshops. The aim was to find a design form that transcended all the genres and that could equally be used in painting, sculpture, the crafts, and architecture. The Rietveld chair uses the universal design elements of the square, the rectangle, and the line all set in a relationship to space. The frame of the chair, a spatial construction, can be completely dismantled into individual planes. In this way, the formal and colour relations of the painterly and sculptural elements continue to apply to an object of everyday use. This is why identical design principles can be used for a book cover, a painting, or a building (Theo van Doesburg, Cornelius van Eesteren, model for the *Maison d'artiste*, 1923).

These basic principles of design form were implemented all over the world by representatives of the Bauhaus. The aim of finding and utilising universal design principles can be seen as having succeeded—an accomplishment of modernism. The global presence of Bauhaus modernism is due to its universal design principles and its research on materials, as well as the use of new materials like glass and metals, the exploration of new formal idioms, and the trend towards transparency. The German Pavilion at the World's Fair in Barcelona in 1929, designed by Ludwig Mies van der Rohe, is seen as a masterpiece of a new vision of space and as an icon of modernism. The floor plan clearly shows the building's innovative and dynamic use of planes. The walls have lost their function as

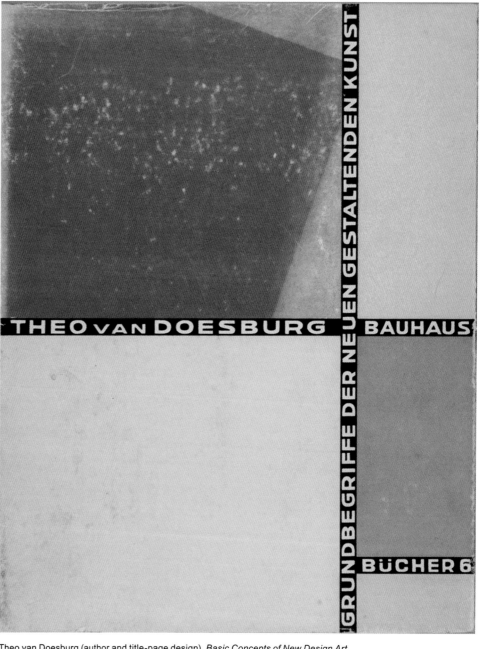

Theo van Doesburg (author and title-page design), *Basic Concepts of New Design Art*, Bauhaus Books no. 6, Munich, 1925

Gerrit Rietveld, *Red and Blue Chair*, c.1918, made by
Gerard van de Groenekan after 1918, painted beechwood,
plywood, Gemeentemuseum Den Haag

László Moholy-Nagy (title-page design), Piet Mondrian, *New Design,*
Bauhaus Books no. 5, Munich, 1925

Theo van Doesburg, Cornelius van Eesteren, Model for the Maison d'artiste, 1923, reconstruction 1983, plexiglas, polystyrene, sticky foil, wood, 60 × 60 × 60 cm, Gemeentemuseum Den Haag

Mies van der Rohe, German Pavilion, Barcelona, 1929, floor plan (based on *Die Form: Zeitschrift für gestaltende Arbeit* 4 [1929], p. 424)

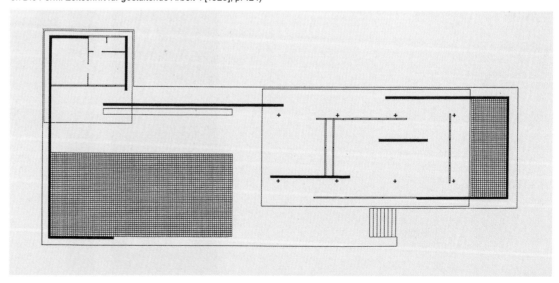

bearers of weight and serve only as dividers, making the floor plan flexible. Mies van der Rohe worked the floor plan by using shifting parts, thus permitting the free structure of architectural elements.

"But what is space, how can it be understood and given a form?"[12] This was the central question put by Walter Gropius in the development of his own concept of architecture and his idea of "an assembly of prefabricated and standardised parts so applied as to fulfil the varying requirements of those to be housed."[13] Gropius's building sets are based on the spatial configuration of the rectangle—linear form is transferred onto a two-dimensional plane. The square in space in turn takes on the form of a cube, leading to a building block. Gropius also creates enhanced three-dimensionality by accumulating and arranging cubes in space. "We want to create a clear, organic architecture, whose inner logic will be radiant and naked, unencumbered by lying facades and trickeries; we want an architecture adapted to our world of machines, radios, and fast motor cars, an architecture whose function is clearly recognisable in the relation of its forms."[14]

Around a hundred years after the foundation of the Bauhaus, new technologies mean that questions of design have entered a new phase. The aesthetic imperative of the Bauhaus, the "unity of art and technology", still applies, but we are now no longer working with analogue machines but with the technology of digital media. Codes have replaced style and form, and algorithms have replaced aesthetics.

In her work *XML-SVG Code / Quellcode des Ausstellungsraums* (2010/2017), artist Karin Sander addresses precisely this digital transformation. In the real space of the ZKM, she makes the architectural data of the exhibition space visible and legible to visitors as written source code. The programming instructions are noted on three walls, processed and graphically transferred by the computer. The XML-SVG code is thus displayed on the walls of the same room whose architectural parameters have created the code—a drawing in a space that is also a drawing of that space.

To date, our culture has been based on a two-dimensional form of notation: writing,

9   Theo van Doesburg, *Grundbegriffe der neuen gestaltenden Kunst*, Bauhaus Books, vol. 6 (Munich, 1925).

10   Naum Gabo, "gestaltung?" in *bauhaus. zeitschrift für gestaltung*, vol. 2 (1928), 4, p. 2 (translated).

11   Theo van Doesburg, "elementarisme", 13 July 1930, in *De Stijl, dernier numero*, 1932, pp. 15–16. Translated in Hans Ludwig C. Jaffé, *Mondrian und De Stijl* (Cologne: Dumont, 1967), pp. 241–2, here 241 (translated).

12   Walter Gropius, *The Theory and Organisation of the Bauhaus* (see note 1).

13   Ibid.

14   Ibid.

15   Sigfried Giedion, *Mechanisation Takes Command: A Contribution to Anonymous History* (New York, 1948).

16   Frank Lloyd Wright, *Modern Architecture: Being the Kahn Lectures for 1930* (Princeton, 1930).

17   Lev Manovich, *Software Takes Command* (New York, 2013).

musical scores, and numbers have been noted and fixed on paper. In the age of digitalisation, the computer makes three-dimensional notation possible. Designs and technical constructions in architecture and design are made today by means of computer-aided design and drafting systems (CAD, CADD). This computer technology allows architects and designers to create dynamic three-dimensional spaces by means of simulation, making it possible to visualise new forms and designs that could not be attained by conventional means. We are the witnesses of a process whereby design is being taken over by the computer and designers are receding ever more into the background. And yet, particularly in co-creation —the collaboration between computer technology (AI algorithms, cloud computing, software) and human decision-making—we are seeing new possibilities for design.
In his book *Mechanisation Takes Command*, Sigfried Giedion described the effects of technological developments on everyday life back in 1948.[15] A major modernist architect, Frank Lloyd Wright, writing in 1930, summarised the equation for the twentieth century after the Bauhaus: "machinery, materials, and men".[16] For the twenty-first century, the equation is: "media, data, and men". Our world is no longer produced just by objects, words, and images, no longer by machines and materials, but above all it is created, guided, and controlled by data. Lev Manovich puts this contemporary state of affairs well: "software takes command" (2013).[17]
Since the Center for Art and Media was opened in Karlsruhe in 1989, its founder-director Heinrich Klotz has often referred to the Dessau Bauhaus, identifying conceptual similarities between the two institutions. The aim to recognise and show the significance of future-oriented media and computer technologies by means of a broad spectrum of artistic and academic approaches is reflected in the main tasks and in the philosophy of the ZKM, which is why it goes by the name of "digital Bauhaus". Whereas in the twentieth century, and in the spirit of the Bauhaus, it was the material design of objects that stood at the centre of artistic exploration, today it is digital design and the codification of data.

Karin Sander, XML-SVG CODE / *Source Code of the Exhibition Space*, 2010/2017, Oracal 638, plotter foil matte, 3-colours, view of the ZKM exhibition *Open Codes*, 2019

Enrique Xavier de Anda Alanís
is an architect with a PhD in art history. He conducts research at the Universidad Nacional Autonoma de México (UNAM) and has published numerous books on modern architecture, including *Luis Barragán 1990: Historia de un debate* (2016) and *Historia de la arquitectura mexicana* (2019, 4th edition). He has received a number of awards, including UNAM's annual prize for his research in the field of architectural history.

Silvia Fernández
is a communication designer and freelance researcher. Since 2008, her research has focused on women and their role in the development of Argentinian design. She co-edited *Historia del Diseño en América Latina y el Caribe* (2008) and is the author of the publication *Señal Bauhaus* (2019). Her articles have appeared in *ulmer modelle – modelle nach ulm: Hochschule für Gestaltung Ulm 1953– 1968* (2003), in *Women's Creativity since the Modern Movement* (2018) and *After Bauhaus, Before Internet* (in press, 2019).

Boris Friedewald
is an independent art historian and author. He is curator of the ifa touring exhibition *The Whole World a Bauhaus* and has published works on art history relating to the Bauhaus, photography, and artist biographies. Together with Magdalena Droste, he was editor of *Our Bauhaus: Memories of Bauhaus People* (2019).

Valérie Hammerbacher
is artistic director of the ifa touring exhibition *The Whole World a Bauhaus* and has been curator at the ifa Gallery in Stuttgart since 2005. She studied art history, philosophy, and literature at the University of Stuttgart and did her PhD on the concept of the image making in the work of photographer Jeff Wall. Her work focuses on contemporary photography and architectural history in the dynamic interface between global art, urban typology, and the development of postcolonial theory. Her most recent publications are *Stuttgart: Architektur des 20. und 21. Jahrhunderts: 22 Stadtspaziergänge* (2013) and *Die Werkbund-siedlung Stuttgart Weißenhof* (2016).

Margret Kentgens-Craig
is adjunct associate professor of architecture at North Carolina State University, USA, and former head of collections and the historical archive at the Bauhaus Dessau Foundation. She is author of numerous publications on the subject of the Bauhaus, including *The Bauhaus and America: First Contacts, 1919– 1936* (MIT Press), and has written for periodicals such as *Appalachian Journal*, *Dezeen*, and *Architectural Record*.

Alexander Klee
has been working at the Belvedere in Vienna since 2010 in his role as curator for the second half of the nineteenth century and the early twentieth century. He is a founding member of the Adolf Hölzel Foundation in Stuttgart and is compiling a complete catalogue of Hölzel's works. His research focuses on the nineteenth century as the beginning of modernism and on the art of classical modernism and post-war modernism in the twentieth century. He curated the exhibitions *Adolf Hölzel und die Wiener Secession* (2007), *Cubism— Constructivism—Form Art* (2016) and *Beyond Klimt: New Horizons in Central Europe* (2018/19).

Salma Lahlou
is a cultural project manager and curator. She has a degree in curatorial studies from Sorbonne University, Paris, and in law from Cardiff University. After working as the vice-president of the National Museums Foundation of Morocco, she founded Thinkart in 2015—an art space for visual arts and curatorial practices in Casablanca. She has curated various exhibitions, the latest being *Loading … Casa* during the Design Week in Dubai (2017) and Brussels (2018), *In the Carpet/Über den Teppich* in Stuttgart (2016) and Berlin (2017), and *The Casablanca School of Fine Arts: Belkahia, Chabâa, Melehi and the Fabrication of Art and History* during the Marrakech Biennale (2016).

David Maulen de los Reyes
is professor at the Metropolitan Technological University (UTEM), Santiago, Chile. Since 1999 he has been conducting research at the interface between art, science, and technology in the context of social change processes in Chile. The direct exchange that took place between Latin America and the Bauhaus and Ulm School of Design in Germany is the subject of many of his articles, including work published in "Collective", the seventh edition of the *Bauhaus* journal (2015), *Revista de arquitectura* 28 (2015), *Bauhaus Imaginista*, online journal (2019), and *100 Jahre Bauhaus: Vielfalt, Konflikt und Wirkung* (2019).

Christiane Post
is a private lecturer at the University of Wuppertal (BUW). She qualified as a professor with her text *Künstlermuseen: Die russische Avantgarde und ihre Museen für Moderne Kunst*. From 2012 to 2016, she was deputy professor at the Academy of Fine Arts in Nuremburg and visiting professor and managing director of the Institute for Art in Context at the Berlin University of the Arts. Her research focuses on the history and theory of art between the nineteenth and twenty-first centuries and the international avant-garde.

Judith Raum
is an artist and author. She studied fine arts and philosophy in Frankfurt am Main and New York. Her multimedia installations and lecture performances focus on the confluence of artistic and scientific (cognitive) formats. She explores topics from social and economic history on the basis of detailed archival research. Since 2016, her focus has been on the Bauhaus textile workshop and the interconnection between textile as a medium and its specific materiality, viewed through the lens of social and industrial history. Her work has manifested, for example, in the installations *Bauhausraum* (2017), Kunsthaus Dresden, and *Stoffbesprechung* (2019), GRASSI Museum of Applied Arts, Leipzig.

Robin Rehm
is a research assistant at the Institute of Art History at the University of Regensburg. His research focuses on the painting of the seventeenth to twentieth centuries, the history and theory of architecture, and the scientific history of colour theory, physiological optics, and psychology. He is the author and editor of numerous texts, including *Das Bauhausgebäude in Dessau: Die ästhetischen Kategorien Zweck Form Inhalt* (2005) and *Designpatente der Moderne: 1840–1970* (2019).

Elisa Tamaschke
is an art historian and curator. She has worked as a research assistant at the Institute for Art History and European Archaeology at the Martin Luther University in Halle (Saale) and at the Georg Kolbe Museum, Berlin. She has published on numerous topics in twentieth- and twenty-first-century art. Together with Magdalena Droste, she is editor of the correspondence between Oskar Schlemmer and Otto Meyer-Amden (2019).

Christoph Wagner
teaches in the Department of Art History at the University of Regensburg. His research on modernist art has won him international acclaim. He is an elected member of the Academia Europaea in London and has been a visiting professor at the École Pratique des Hautes Études in Paris, the University of Bern, and the UNAM University of Mexico. As a scholar and curator, he made a name for himself with the exhibitions *Bauhaus and the Esoteric* and *Itten—Klee: Cosmos of Color*. He is currently publishing the catalogue raisonné of the work of Johannes Itten.

Peter Weibel
Peter Weibel has been chairman and executive director of the ZKM | Center for Art and Media Karlsruhe since 1999. His diverse activities as an artist, media theorist, curator, and nomad migrating between art and science, as a teacher at universities and long-term director of institutions such as Ars Electronica, Linz, and the Institute for New Media in Frankfurt am Main, have made him a key figure in European media art.

Image credits

El mundo entero es una Bauhaus
22 June – 12 August 2018
MUSEO NACIONAL DE ARTE DECORATIVO,
BUENOS AIRES, ARGENTINA

El mundo entero es una Bauhaus
29 October – 14 December 2018
MUSEO UNIVERSITARIO DE CIENCIAS Y
ARTE, MEXICO CITY, MEXICO

The Whole World a Bauhaus
23 February – 21 April 2019
ELMHURST ART MUSEUM, ILLINOIS, USA

El mundo entero es una Bauhaus
19 June – 18 August 2019
MUSEO MUNICIPAL DE BELLAS ARTES
"JUAN MANUEL BLANES", MONTEVIDEO,
URUGUAY

pp. 189–191
Exhibition views
MUSEO NACIONAL DE ARTE DECORATIVO,
BUENOS AIRES, ARGENTINA

EL HOMBRE NUEVO

Exhibition view
MUSEO UNIVERSITARIO DE CIENCIAS Y
ARTE, MEXICO CITY, MEXICO

Exhibition view
MUSEO MUNICIPAL DE BELLAS ARTES "JUAN MANUEL BLANES",
MONTEVIDEO, URUGUAY

Colophon

This book has been published on the occasion of the exhibition
The Whole World a Bauhaus

The exhibition premiered in Germany at the ZKM | Center for Art and Media Karlsruhe

26 October 2019 – 16 February 2020

The exhibition was organized by ifa (Institut für Auslandsbeziehungen) Stuttgart, Germany
www.ifa.de

Based in Stuttgart and Berlin, ifa (Institut für Auslandsbeziehungen) is Germany's oldest intermediary organization for international cultural and educational relations. It was founded in 1917 as the German Foreign Institute in Stuttgart, and today runs programs that bring together people in the sciences, media, politics, and civil society. Working globally, ifa promotes new encounters and collaborations among those whose cultural practice engages with art and media.

Director
Ellen Strittmatter

Art Director
Valérie Hammerbacher

Project Manager
Clea Laade

Research Assistance
Laura Wünsche
Lara Eva Sochor
Elena Steinemann
Elena Kaifel
Stefanie Bürgel

The exhibition The Whole World a Bauhaus was supported by:

State Ministry of Baden-Württemberg for Science, Research, and the Arts

ZKM | Center for Art and Media Karlsruhe

Artistic-Scientific Chairman, CEO
Peter Weibel

Head of Curatorial Department
Philipp Ziegler

Project Manager
Hannah-Maria Winters

Technical Manager
Anne Däuper

Exhibition

Curator – Touring Exhibition
Boris Friedewald

Section Curators – The Global Bauhaus
Enrique X. de Anda Alanís: Mexico City, Mexico
Silvia Fernández: Buenos Aires, Argentina
Margret Kentgens-Craig: Reception of the Bauhaus in the USA, 1919–1939, Raleigh, USA
Alexander Klee: Stuttgart, Germany
Salma Lahlou: Casablanca, Morocco
David Maulen: Santiago de Chile, Chile
Christiane Post: Moscow, Russia

Section Curator – ZKM | Center for Art and Media Karlsruhe
Peter Weibel

Biographical Texts
Boris Friedewald
Astrid Volpert

Installation Design and Architecture
Studio Ilke Penzlien with
Peter Kortmann
and Robert Müller

Technical Director
Martin Edelmann

With the kind support of:
Ingrid L. Blecha Gesellschaft m.b.H., Filmolux
Deutschland GmbH, KPM Königliche Porzel-
lan-Manufaktur Berlin GmbH, Christopher
Farr, Mevaco GmbH, Tecnolumen GmbH &
Co. KG, Naef Spiele AG, Dringenberg GmbH

Catalogue

Published by
Hirmer Verlag
Bayerstraße 57–59
80335 Munich
www.hirmerpublishers.com

Editor
ifa (Institut für Auslandsbeziehungen)

Copyediting and Proofreading
James Copeland, Berlin

Translation from the German
Simon Cowper, Tsagkarada
Greg Bond, Berlin
Gérard Goodrow, Cologne

Photography
Andreas Körner, bildhübsche Fotografie,
Stuttgart

Chronology and Diagram
Nicole Opel, Berlin

Graphic Design and Layout
HIT, Berlin

Project Management – Hirmer Verlag
Cordula Gielen

Production – Hirmer Verlag
Hannes Halder

Pre-press and Repro
Reproline Genceller GmbH & Co. KG, Munich

Printing and Binding
Westermann Druck GmbH, Zwickau

Printed in Germany

© 2019 Institut für Auslandsbeziehungen e. V.
(ifa); Hirmer Verlag GmbH, Munich; the artists
and authors

Bibliographic information published by
the Deutsche Nationalbibliothek
The Deutsche Nationalbibliothek lists
this publication in the Deutsche National-
bibliografie; detailed bibliographic data
is available online at http://dnb.de.

ISBN
Trade edition
978-3-7774-3416-2 (German)
978-3-7774-3417-9 (English)

ISBN
ifa-edition
978-3-948205-06-5 (German)
978-3-948205-10-2 (English)

Frontispiece, pp. 42, 94: Rasch Co.,
three samples of Bauhaus wallpapers,
designed by students of the Bauhaus, 1932